New perspectives in local governance

Reviewing the research evidence

**Howard Davis & Chris Skelcher,
Michael Clarke, Marilyn Taylor,
Ken Young & Nirmala Rao,
Gerry Stoker**

With an introduction by Robin Hambleton

The **Joseph Rowntree Foundation** has supported this project as part of its programme of research and innovative development projects, which it hopes will be of value to policy makers and practitioners. The facts presented and views expressed in this study are, however, those of the authors and not necessarily those of the Foundation.

The contributors

Professor Robin Hambleton is Associate Dean (Research and Consultancy) in the Faculty of the Built Environment, University of the West of England, Bristol. He is a member of the Local and Central Government Relations Research Committee of the Joseph Rowntree Foundation.

Howard Davis is a Lecturer at the School of Public Policy, The University of Birmingham.

Chris Skelcher is a Senior Lecturer at the School of Public Policy, The University of Birmingham.

Michael Clarke is Professor of Public Policy and Head of the School of Public Policy, The University of Birmingham.

Marilyn Taylor is a Reader in Social Policy at the University of Brighton.

Nirmala Rao is a Lecturer in Politics at Goldsmith's College, University of London.

Ken Young is Professor of Politics and Vice-Principal at Queen Mary and Westfield College, University of London.

Gerry Stoker is Professor of Politics at the University of Strathclyde. He is a member of the Local and Central Government Relations Research Committee of the Joseph Rowntree Foundation.

Acknowledgements

Thanks are due to Kathy Bonehill for support with Chapter 1, and to Simon Braunholtz at MORI for helpful comments on Chapter 4.

Published by YPS for the Joseph Rowntree Foundation

ISBN 1 899987 26 6

Prepared and printed by:
York Publishing Services Ltd
64 Hallfield Road
Layerthorpe, York YO3 7XQ

Contents

Introduction and overview

Robin Hambleton

The Joseph Rowntree Foundation has funded a major programme of research on
the relations between local and central government. In the years since the Local
and Central Government Relations Research Committee was set up in 1988, over
60 research reports have been published. Sir Charles Carter, the Chairman of the
Research Committee, has written a book bringing together many of the findings
of this body of work under the title *Members One of Another: the Problems of Local
Corporate Action* (Carter, 1996).

When the Research Committee first started looking at relations between local
and central government, the focus of attention was on institutional roles and
relationships, for example the financial relationship. For a variety of reasons
these roles and relationships have been changing rapidly in recent years. The
political context within which the institutions of local and central government
operate has also moved on. The Research Committee responded to these
changes by widening its perspective to consider a range of issues relating to the
changing nature of local governance. The committee was well aware of a
number of parallel research programmes managed by other organisations –
notably the Economic and Social Research Council, the Local Government
Management Board, the Commission for Local Democracy, the Department of
the Environment and the Audit Commission. Steps were taken to ensure that
research commissioned by the Joseph Rowntree Foundation would not
duplicate work funded by other bodies.

To help pull together the main findings of recent research on local governance,
the Research Committee commissioned a series of five 'synthesis papers'. These
papers – which bring together findings from a variety of research programmes,
not just those funded by the Joseph Rowntree Foundation – are brought together
in this volume. The chapters review research on:

- QUANGOs

- the new public management

- the impact of local government changes on the voluntary and community
  sectors

- public attitudes to local government

- local political participation.

Each chapter sets out to review relevant published and, where possible, unpublished research findings and to identify and interpret key themes arising from the research. In addition, each chapter reflects on the lessons from the research for local/central relations and for current and future policies relating to local government. The five topics are all significant for the future development of local/central relations and for local governance, and the synthesis papers have been most helpful to the Research Committee. It was felt that they should be made available to a wider audience – hence this book. The authors of each chapter develop their own distinctive analysis so that the book is best viewed as a collection of free-standing essays which bring together insights on the very latest research evidence. Each chapter also acts as a guide to the relevant published literature so that the book provides a useful research resource. This Introduction provides a brief overview of some of the major themes to emerge from each analysis.

The fragmentation of local governance

Research on QUANGOs suggests that the monolithic local authority, controlling and managing the vast bulk of local policy-making and public service delivery, is a thing of the past. Many of the public services which affect electors are now outside local democratic control. Health, training, urban regeneration and further education are among the services which are now the responsibility of appointed, rather than elected, bodies. In Chapter 1, Howard Davis and Chris Skelcher explore this 'twilight world' in which major public policy decisions are made in private by largely unknown board members. They tread warily for they recognise at the outset that much of the published material on QUANGOs is specifically directed at shaping public or political opinion.

Introducing a theme which is also discussed by Michael Clarke in Chapter 2, the authors suggest that the growth of QUANGOs is fragmenting local policy-making. Fragmentation, they argue, reduces the capacity of the system of governance to deal with issues that require an integrated approach at the local level. Sustainable development, safer communities, public health, and equal opportunities are just some of the important policy challenges facing local governance that cry out for effective policy co-ordination at the local level. QUANGOisation has improved 'vertical' integration between local and central levels within services but the research suggests that it has damaged 'horizontal' working between local departments and agencies.

One effect of the growth of QUANGOs is that decision-making on key aspects of many public services has become highly centralised. Davis and Skelcher point out that this brings with it potential problems of overload for central government. As ultimate decider and arbiter on an ever-increasing range of issues, the centre is in danger of getting bogged down in the detail of local decision-making. Here, then, is an argument for decentralising power to local authorities not just because it enhances democratic accountability but because it enhances the ability of central government to deal with strategic rather than detailed issues.

There is now a growing body of work on QUANGOs in operation, on the appointment methods used by QUANGOs, and on the arrangements for holding QUANGOs to account. This research shows that there are considerable differences between types of local appointed bodies. Indeed, there is disagreement on how to define what a QUANGO is in the first place. It follows that it is dangerous to generalise too freely about the performance of QUANGOs.

Much of the work does show, however, that members of the business community hold a sizeable proportion of seats on QUANGOs; that there have been a series of cases of financial mismanagement by QUANGOs; and that decision-making procedures in QUANGOs are relatively secretive. A key theme in research has concerned accountability. There have been many critical reports, with one study concluding that the 'current arrangements for accountability are so confused and contradictory as to be probably unsustainable' (Plummer, 1994).

The new public management

We should beware of thinking of the 'new public management' as a single model of organisation – it assumes different forms in different nations according to their political, economic and cultural conditions. For example, a recent US contribution to these debates puts particular emphasis on entrepreneurial forms of management (Osborne and Gaebler, 1992). Within the UK the new public management has been, and will be, shaped into different styles in different policy areas, at different levels of government, under different forms of political control.

In Chapter 2, Michael Clarke recognises this diversity and argues that there has not been a paradigm shift from public 'administration' to public 'management' during the last couple of decades. This is not to imply that changes in management thinking and practice in the public services have been marginal in this period, but to argue that there has been a change of emphasis rather than a revolution. Many of the management innovations of the 1970s and 1980s (for example, policy planning and performance review) live on in the new public management, while others (for example, elaborate corporate plans) have gone and new elements (notably market models and competition) have arrived.

Clarke identifies a number of important themes in research on aspects of the new public management. The growth of competitive models and the emergence of a contract culture have had a major impact on approaches to management in local government. There have been gains in cost effectiveness, but the invaluable study of market mechanisms by Walsh (1995) suggests that the formal processes of competitive tendering, as imposed by central government legislation, do not emulate the practices often found in the private sector. He highlights the importance of informal relationships between client and contractor and the development of trust – not least to allow for flexibility, adaptability and learning.

Competition and markets are seen as having contributed to the fragmentation of local government. Alongside the QUANGOisation of public services referred to earlier, steps have been taken to disaggregate large public service organisations into smaller units. This puts new pressures on local authorities to provide clear policy frameworks for the disaggregated units and to foster effective collaborative action with other agencies. New research suggests that innovative local authorities are responding to this challenge (Hambleton, Hoggett and Razzaque, 1996). Clarke rightly argues that skills in partnership working can be expected to be increasingly valued in the future.

Politicians and managers who recognise the limitations of market models in a public service context have seen the potential of using the new public management to empower citizens and communities. There is a link to be made here between the managerial innovations which empower local managers and front line staff, and the political innovations, described by Gerry Stoker in Chapter 5, which seek to strengthen public involvement in decision-making.

The results of research on performance management seem to be equivocal. Clarke notes that efficiency measures have shown improvement but the causation is often difficult to establish – is it new patterns of management, or additional resources, or something else which makes the difference? Research on change management suggests, however, that local authority political leaders and chief executives are, in some areas at least, showing that they are capable of using external pressures to re-shape their organisations to meet locally defined purpose. It remains the case, however, that local authorities are constrained by legal barriers when it comes to radical organisational change. This problem has received attention in recent cross-national research for the local authority associations and the Commission for Local Democracy (Hambleton and Bullock, 1996; Stoker, 1996). Both these studies advocate new legislation, to give space for local authorities to try out new models, and new incentives to encourage local authorities to put themselves forward as exemplars.

Local government and the voluntary/community sectors

The language of the new public management – enabling, contracting, partnership – points up new challenges for welfare, voluntary and community organisations. Government policies require voluntary bodies to shoulder new roles in service delivery. At the same time there are currents of change seeking to widen community involvement in public debate and local decision-making. In Chapter 3, Marilyn Taylor discusses both these sets of changes in turn. First of all she considers how recent changes have affected the role of community and voluntary organisations as 'partners in service'. Then she examines the impact on their political role as 'partners in policy-making'.

The majority of the research reviewed by Taylor relates to two fields – social care and urban regeneration. These are, in themselves, very important areas of local government responsibility. However, the research also signals themes and issues of relevance to other fields. In relation to the 'partners in service' theme, two key issues are raised for the voluntary sector:

- capacity – how equipped are voluntary and community organisations to take on new roles? Who are the winners and losers? What are the costs and benefits?

- control – who will determine the future role, shape and operations of voluntary and community organisations?

Taylor argues that smaller and medium-sized voluntary organisations are at a considerable disadvantage in the new market-based environment and that, even if they survive, they do so in conditions of insecurity and instability. The larger players or not-for-profits floated off from statutory providers are likely to dominate. It follows that local authorities need to become better informed about their local voluntary and community sector so that they can relate effectively to the smaller organisations which are often particularly successful in meeting unmet needs. This is especially important for excluded groups such as ethnic minority organisations. Taylor fears, however, that the financial frameworks imposed by central government act as significant disincentives to market development even in areas where a viable market could emerge, such as in home care.

In relation to the 'partners in policy-making' theme, Taylor correctly notes that public participation in service and area planning is nothing new. However, central government has introduced new requirements relating to consultation with voluntary, community and service user organisations, and most recently in Local Agenda 21 discussions. This emphasis on partnership working is, as mentioned by Michael Clarke in Chapter 2, likely to grow. Research suggests that partnership working can lead to lasting benefits. For example, if residents help to shape their local environment they can be expected to invest in maintaining it in the future.

Taylor notes, however, that the research to date suggests that, while access for outsiders to policy networks may have improved, the influence of voluntary and community organisations remains that of 'peripheral' insider (Maloney *et al.*, 1994). One key theme to emerge from the research concerns the cultural differences between prospective partners. For example, research on urban regeneration suggests that it is usually the community that has to adjust rather than the public service organisations.

In closing her analysis, Taylor notes that there is an unhelpful separation between the social and public policy research communities and the voluntary sector research community. Even within voluntary sector studies there seems to be little communication, for example, between those studying environmental, arts and social welfare organisations. She rightly argues for greater cross-fertilisation and an enhanced contribution from the mainstream disciplines of sociology and political science.

Public attitudes to local government

There is now a good deal of material available on public attitudes to local government. In Chapter 4, Ken Young and Nirmala Rao provide a review of some of the main findings to emerge from this work. Supported by 37 tables, the chapter provides numerous detailed insights on public awareness, understandings and feelings. The authors point out that studies have been carried out on the attitudes of many interested parties – local authority employees, MPs, civil servants, councillors and members of appointed boards. Here, however, the focus is on public attitudes to local government as derived (mainly) from five major, comparable national studies carried out at various times between 1965 and 1994.

Do public attitudes matter? Young and Rao argue that they are critical – not least because they provide the foundations for the institutions of local democracy. At one level the case for taking public attitudes seriously can be related to survival – if citizens are indifferent or hostile to local government its continued existence can be called into question. More positively it can be argued that the listening local authority which learns about public perceptions and takes them seriously is armed with the information to improve service and policy responsiveness. On this analysis public attitudes are central not just to the enhancement of service quality but also to the whole way the local authority projects itself to the wider world.

The working of local democracy is predicated upon the well-informed citizen who understands local affairs and knows who is responsible for what services. On the criterion of awareness and knowledge, the research evidence presented in Chapter 4 is reasonably comforting. Levels of public knowledge of who provides services is high, for example 70 per cent for schools and 77 per cent for street cleaning. Knowledge of the financing of council services is also relatively high. Seven out of ten respondents could name their local council. Party politics is more vigorous in the more urban areas and knowledge of which party controls the council is, not surprisingly, higher in urban areas. There are important variations across the country and between different age groups. For example, the oldest and youngest are less knowledgeable than the middle aged.

The evidence presented on public satisfaction with local authorities leaves no room for complacency. Overall satisfaction levels have increased in the period from 1991 to 1995 with 61 per cent agreeing that the quality of local council services is good overall in the more recent survey. Young and Rao show that figures of this kind give a superficial picture. Thus, service use has a dramatic impact on service satisfaction, for example in 1995 only 54 per cent were satisfied with primary schools. However, when those without a primary school-aged child in the household were filtered out the figure rose to 81 per cent. This will be comforting to those responsible for delivering local government services.

Evidence assessing the attachment to local government seems to have remained fairly stable over the years. Interestingly, Table 20 suggests that in 1994 28 per cent of Conservative supporters favoured less central government control of local government. Some 48 per cent of Labour and 46 per cent of Liberal supporters took this view. Perhaps there is a broader base of support for more power to local government than has been widely recognised by many politicians and the media.

Unfortunately, the level of voter turnout in local elections does not compare very well with other European countries, although it is better than the USA. One of the most alarming findings is the steep and continuing decline in people's belief that local elections decide how things are run locally. This has slumped from 77 per cent in 1965 to 54 per cent in 1994.

Young and Rao present a rich array of data on public attitudes but they also throw in a word of caution in relation to the measurement of satisfaction. Generalised 'satisfaction with the local council' questions may be tapping into a still more general 'satisfaction with life' dimension.

Local political participation

The evidence assembled by Gerry Stoker in Chapter 5 complements the analysis presented by Ken Young and Nirmala Rao. Both chapters start from the premise that citizen participation is fundamental to the operation of democratic government. Chapter 4 includes, as we have seen, some discussion of voting patterns and also presents some data on whether citizens would be willing to protest local government actions (Tables 15–18). Chapter 5 provides an extended discussion of participation. It addresses some fundamental questions – Who participates? Why participate? – and reviews a wide range of participation mechanisms, from voting through to the use of information and communication technologies.

Stoker notes that, whilst official interest in public participation shot up in the late 1960s and early 1970s, it would be wrong to imagine that this era represented a golden age of participation with respect to local government. Perhaps the period is best viewed as a time when there was a significant shift beyond the representative model – new opportunities for public involvement were opened up and a good deal of experimentation and learning took place. Interest in participation certainly declined in the 1980s at the height of the New Right agenda. However, it is possible to argue, as Stoker does, that the 1990s have seen a renewal of interest in participation. Some of the reasons for this resurgence are identified by Clarke and Taylor in earlier chapters.

The survey data suggests that participation of an extensive nature is a minority activity – perhaps a quarter of the population are activists. Around half the population vote but don't do much else. The remaining quarter might be regarded as 'almost inactive'. These figures give the impression that the vast majority appear to be passive or disaffected. However, the figures also show that nearly 10 million people are relatively active nationally – a significant number by any standards.

Activists tend to be better educated, wealthier and better networked, but closer analysis shows that different groups of activists have distinctive social profiles. Also the evidence suggests that participation varies across localities. In other words, local studies suggest that in different areas local leadership, culture and organisations can enhance the propensity of citizens to participate.

Stoker examines various rationales for participation, from self-interested behaviour through to deliberative democracy. The latter is built on the premise that politics should involve reasoning, open debate and reflection on the opinions of others. The discussion of voting and non-voting amplifies the concerns expressed by Young and Rao – people appear to be losing faith in local elections.

In the remainder of Chapter 5, Stoker reviews officially-sponsored participation mechanisms (of which there are now many), assesses the role of non-governmental forms of participation and outlines some recent innovations, for example referenda and citizens' juries. In debates about public involvement there is sometimes an unhelpful polarisation between those who defend existing representative forms of local democracy and those who advocate more participatory forms. Stoker rightly argues that the challenge is not necessarily to replace established forms of participation, rather it is to explore how a variety of approaches can, in combination, enhance the quality of local democracy.

Conclusion

It is clear that a large amount of research on the institutions of local governance has been carried out in recent years. This collection of essays on different themes does not offer a comprehensive assessment of all this research. In particular, those interested in the specific agenda of local/central relations would be well advised to refer to the separate publication referred to earlier (Carter, 1996). The collection does, however, offer a useful gathering together of diverse research materials and it is hoped that it will be useful to scholars, practitioners and students and, indeed, all those concerned to develop a better understanding of the challenges facing local governance in the 1990s.

References

Carter, Sir Charles (1996) *Members One of Another: the Problems of Local Corporate Action*. York: Joseph Rowntree Foundation

Hambleton, R. and Bullock, S. (1996) *Revitalising Local Democracy. The Leadership Options*. London: Association of District Councils/Local Government Management Board

Hambleton, R., Hoggett, P. and Razzaque, K. (1996) *Freedom Within Boundaries. Developing Effective Approaches to Decentralisation*. London: Local Government Management Board

Maloney, W.J., Jordan, G. and McLaughlin, A. (1994) 'Interest groups and public policy: the insider/outsider model revisited', *Journal of Public Policy*, vol. 14, no. 1, pp. 17–38

Osborne, D. and Gaebler, T. (1992) *Reinventing Government*. New York: Plume

Plummer, J. (1994) *The Governance Gap: QUANGOs and Accountability*. London: LGC Communications and Joseph Rowntree Foundation

Stoker, G. (1996) *The Reform of the Institutions of Local Representative Democracy: Is There a Role for the Mayor–Council Model?* Research Report No. 18. London: Commission for Local Democracy

Walsh, K. (1995) *Public Services and Market Mechanisms*. London: Macmillan

1 Reviewing QUANGOs: A research synthesis

Howard Davis and Chris Skelcher

Introduction and overview

Many of the public services which affect electors are now being provided by agencies over which they have no direct democratic control. Health, training, urban regeneration and further education are among the services which are now the responsibility of appointed, rather than elected, bodies. The policies of these appointed bodies, and the services they provide, have a significant impact on people's lives, yet they exist in a twilight world with many of their decisions made in private and their board members unknown. This has generated much research interest.

Research on the non-elected sector of government, generally referred to as QUANGOs, falls into a number of categories. Firstly, there are academic studies – often quite substantial pieces of work – which use a social science methodology to investigate and draw conclusions about particular aspects of the sector. These frequently involve primary research that generates new data. Secondly, there are shorter 'quick and dirty' analyses that seek either to inform the current debate about non-elected bodies or undertake a preliminary investigation of a specific question. For the most part these draw on secondary sources, some of which, until then, may not have been collated. These include studies by academic institutions, independent research bodies and the media. Thirdly, there are studies by politicians and political parties which present results directed, in the main, at criticising non-elected bodies and their operation. These frequently make use of Parliamentary Questions to bring new data into the public realm.

The significance of the non-elected sector in the public policy agenda means that a large number of articles and reports have been published in recent years. A comprehensive annotated bibliography and survey of the published literature on QUANGOs has been produced by Grayson and Davis (1996). Compared with many other areas of public policy, research into such bodies needs to be treated with some caution. The methodology and purpose of the study should be understood since many publications have been specifically directed at shaping public or political opinion. We have included these in our review where we believe that they contribute reliable data or understanding, whether or not they have a particular value base.

In this paper we seek to draw out the main themes of the current debate about QUANGOs: determining the boundaries of the appointed sector; appointments and patronage; standards of conduct in public life; the fragmentation of local governance; QUANGOs in operation; and accountability. The Appendix contains an analysis of selected recent research into QUANGOs.

The boundaries of the appointed sector

Determining the extent of the appointed sector is an increasingly difficult issue. Legislatively-imposed or government-inspired changes affecting the provision of public services have led to a blurred and confusing picture. The issue itself may seem mundane yet it is a matter of great controversy. There are many appointed bodies now sharing territory at local level with elected local government (see pp. 17-19) and the underlying point is potentially of great significance, for if it can be argued that an activity is (or is not) appropriate for electoral control, then different arguments may apply, for instance in relation to the appropriate accountability arrangements and standards of conduct.

The definition of the appointed sector is also contested. Government tends to take a tighter, narrower view than others – referring to Non-Departmental Public Bodies (NDPBs) and health service bodies only. This leads to the wide discrepancies in the number of QUANGOs cited by the government (e.g. in *Public Bodies*, annually) and by those making the counter-argument (e.g. Weir and Hall, 1994). Titles also contribute to the confusion. Training and Enterprise Councils (TECs) are not councils in the sense that that term is normally understood. Rather they are constituted as companies limited by guarantee. There are many other examples of misleading usage of titles, such as Housing Action Trusts and NHS trusts – the term 'trust' implying a charitable status that does not match the reality of these bodies. A similar point can be made in relation to the new Education Associations which may be appointed to take over the running of 'failing' schools.

In the end, writers are currently forced to define the boundaries of the appointed sector for themselves, usually with a large element of pragmatism (see, for instance, Davis and Stewart, 1993; Painter *et al.*, 1994; Skelcher and Davis, 1995). Often there is a core of agreement, so that most writers tend to include Training and Enterprise Councils within their definition. There is much greater controversy about housing associations. Weir and Hall (1994) include housing associations in their area of search. Klein and Day (undated) argue differently. Davis and Spencer (1995) are somewhere in-between.

The second stage of the Nolan Committee's work (Committee on Standards in Public Life, 1995b; 1996), concerning 'local public spending bodies', touches on these arguments. The Committee has produced its own operational definition. 'Local public spending bodies' are defined by the Committee (1995b) as 'bodies which are neither fully elected nor appointed by ministers, but which provide public services, often delivered at local level, which are wholly or largely publicly funded'. The Nolan Committee is unable to challenge the constitutional base of such bodies 'head on' but has sought to establish an appropriate working definition in order that it may proceed with its work on standards in public life. The Committee has included housing associations (amongst other bodies) within its area of search.

Appointments and patronage

The question of how individuals come to be appointed to QUANGOs is not a new one. Weir and Hall (1994) comment on patronage by the 1974–79 Labour government and a number of studies were undertaken at the time (for example, Doig, 1977). These note the informality and closed nature of the process and its use to gain party political advantage in non-elected areas of government. Recently the issue has resurfaced. Studies have been undertaken either through analysis of official documents and records or by surveying and interviewing appointees themselves. These methods have advantages on pragmatic grounds, in the sense that researchers are probably more easily able to gain access to board members than those managing and making decisions on appointments – particularly in central government. However, the disadvantage is that it produces data from only one of the parties involved and may require respondents to make assumptions about why they were selected.

In terms of the local appointed sector, Davis and Stewart (1993) examine the appointment methods and criteria applying to a range of bodies – to the extent that these methods and criteria can be identified. They conclude that these bodies broadly divide into two groups – those appointed by a minister or an intermediary body appointed by a minister, and those that are wholly or largely self-appointing. A wide variety of methods and criteria are used in the latter case. This mapping study is complemented by detailed research into appointments to particular bodies or groups of bodies. A survey of eight local appointed bodies, covering some 1,500 non-executive members, highlighted the significance of existing board members and senior executives as the source of nominations for appointments (Skelcher and Davis, 1995). Such word-of-mouth recruitment was preferred by members. The research concluded that this was one factor leading to similarities in the socio-economic backgrounds of members on local appointed bodies and would be likely to result in members' values being similar. A survey of health authority and NHS trust non-executives reached a similar finding (Ashburner and Cairncross, 1993). It noted the considerable patronage available to the Secretary of State and to the chairs of health authorities and trusts, and drew attention to the desire of government to appoint individuals with business experience. This pattern is also reflected in studies of Further and Higher Education College governors (Bastin, 1990; Graystone, 1991) where, as in TECs, a proportion of board places are reserved for employers.

Studies of particular localities have begun to explore the linkages between appointed body memberships – and particularly the chairs of boards – and the local business and political elite. Research in London (Colenutt and Ellis, 1993); the North East of England (Robinson and Shaw, 1994); Wales (Morgan and Roberts, 1993; Morgan and Osmond, 1995); and the West Midlands (Davis, 1993; Painter et al., 1994) indicates that local appointed bodies are closely integrated into the networks of power in the area. The informality of many appointment processes facilitates this interlinkage and ensures that it remains hidden from public view.

National and regional bodies with executive and advisory functions are examined in Weir and Hall (1994) and Hall and Weir (1995). Their analysis highlights the potential for patronage through ministerial control of the appointment process, and the role of the Public Appointments Unit in gathering and evaluating potential appointees. These issues have been examined in relation to Wales by Morgan and Roberts (1993). They note that the territorial focus of the Secretary of State for Wales enables him to exercise patronage over a much wider range of QUANGOs than Cabinet colleagues responsible for English ministries. In Scotland, by contrast, there is an established system through which individuals can apply to be considered for non-executive positions on health service and some other boards. A panel considers these and advises the Secretary of State (Midwinter, 1995).

Patronage and political bias
The closed nature of the appointment process and the exercise of patronage has generated a considerable public debate about whether QUANGOs are packed with the Government's supporters. Some limited research has investigated this

question. Hall and Weir (1995) and Morgan and Osmond (1995) both provide political and business biographies of the members of a number of regional and national QUANGOs. Robinson and Shaw (1994) undertake a similar task for regional and local QUANGOs in North East England, Davis (1994) for the West Midlands and the Labour Research Department (1994) for the health service nationally. The largest piece of primary research in this area is that undertaken by Alan Milburn, MP and Peter Kilfoyle, MP in association with the BBC *Here and Now* programme. Using Parliamentary Questions, Kilfoyle and Milburn obtained the names of the members of each Non-Departmental Public Body (BBC, 1994a, 1994b, 1994c). This was used by the BBC to identify individuals holding multiple appointments. The names were also compared with board members of companies supporting the Conservative and Labour Parties and other individuals known to have party affiliations. The conclusion that can be drawn from this research is that an individual has a greater chance of holding an appointment to a QUANGO if they have connections to the Conservative Party rather than the Labour Party. These connections may be through membership of the Conservative Party or being a board member of a company that donates to party funds.

Despite the size of the Milburn/Kilfoyle/BBC data set, the conclusions are based on a small number of cases. This is because of problems associated with identifying individuals' political affiliations. The first is that secondary sources of data on individuals' party political affiliations are either not available or sparse. The second is that membership or support for a particular political party does not necessarily mean that an individual will align themselves with that party's current policy or decisions. Patronage does not necessarily create compliant board members.

The characteristics of appointees
Members of local appointed bodies are predominantly white, male, well educated, from professional or managerial occupations and aged over 45 (Skelcher and Davis, 1995). In this respect they reflect the characteristics of those holding other positions of power in British society. No comparable research has been undertaken into the membership characteristics of national and regional QUANGOs but, from the evidence available (e.g. Hall and Weir, 1995), a broadly similar picture would be expected to emerge. There are, however, considerable differences between types of local appointed body. Health service boards and Housing Action Trusts have a higher proportion of women members; Housing Action Trusts have a higher proportion of Black and Asian members; and City Challenge boards have a younger profile than other bodies. These differences

arise in part from the appointment methods and criteria, for example the policy to increase the number of women who are health service non-executive board members (Ashburner and Cairncross, 1993).

Members of the business community hold a sizeable proportion of seats on QUANGOs, partly in response to the Government's desire to apply their values and skills to the public service. Early research on the new Police Authorities confirms that this bias has been repeated amongst the 'independent' members of those authorities (Loveday, 1995). However, the way they see their role, the impact they have and their relationship to their 'constituency' remains an area where limited research has been conducted (e.g. Peck, 1993). The same is true of community representatives on Housing Action Trusts and City Challenge. Again some initial research has explored their experience (e.g. MacFarlane, 1993).

Standards of conduct

There has been an unfortunate catalogue of failings by a number of appointed public bodies. Among the best-known examples of failure are the misuse of public funds by the Welsh Development Agency, managerial shortcomings in the Wessex and West Midlands Regional Health Authorities, and the spectacular collapse of the London Ambulance Service's computerised mobilising system. There has been a succession of official reports on these many and varied happenings.

In January 1994, the House of Commons Committee of Public Accounts produced an omnibus report on *The Proper Conduct of Public Business* bringing together the key findings of a number of the Committee's own inquiries. The report begins with the following words:

> *In recent years we have seen and reported on a number of serious failures in administrative and financial systems and controls within departments and other public bodies, which have led to money being wasted or otherwise improperly spent. These failings represent a departure from the standards of public conduct which have mainly been established during the past 140 years.*

Alongside other unrelated scandals, the continuing concern and allegations about QUANGOs led to an atmosphere of sleaze enveloping government. The government's main response was to appoint a Committee on Standards in Public Life, in October 1994, to investigate the issue and seek to restore public confidence. The Committee is chaired by the judge Lord Nolan. The first report of the committee was published in May 1995 and sets out seven principles of public life together with some 55 specific recommendations aimed at ensuring high standards of behaviour and probity in public life and reducing the scope for patronage. A number of concerns raised by academic writers (e.g. Stewart and Davis, 1994; Skelcher and Davis, 1995; Wright, 1995) are addressed.

However, the terms of reference of the Nolan Committee are limited to issues relating to standards of conduct and do not extend to the rights and wrongs of, for instance, the existence of appointed bodies as a way of running public services. There are also arguments that the response to concerns about falling standards in public life is inadequate (see, for example, Davis and Daly, 1995). Nolan's second report (Committee on Standards in Public Life, 1996) examines standards of conduct in what the committee has termed 'local public spending bodies' which include further education colleges, grant maintained schools, universities, housing associations and Training and Enterprise Councils. Lord Nolan comments that 'Nothing in [the] report points to any fundamental malaise in any of the sectors which we have examined. But there is, and will continue to be, a tension between the management driven and output related approach which is central to many recent changes, and the need for organisations providing public services to involve, respond to, and reflect the concerns of the communities which they serve.' The principle of unpaid voluntary service was strongly reaffirmed by the Committee.

These various official enquiries have proved invaluable in addressing aspects of public concern about standards of conduct.

The fragmentation of local governance

Fragmentation has become a commonplace concern within local government. The concern is with the rapid growth in the number of appointed bodies responsible for public services and operating at the local level, often supplanting elected local government (Davis and Stewart, 1993; Weir and Hall, 1994; etc.). Davis and Stewart undertook initial 'mapping' research for the Local Government Management Board (LGMB) in 1993. They comment that, 'The reality is that there are now two systems of government at local level and two sets of members – one elected and the other appointed.' This has been complemented recently by further work for the LGMB (Leach *et al.*, 1996) where the following definition is given:

Fragmentation is differentiation which lacks compensatory integration.

The concern is that the fragmentation of responsibilities away from local government to a range of appointed bodies is reducing the capacity to deal with issues that require different functions or institutions to work together.

The Leach *et al.* study identifies three different types of body now 'sharing the turf' with the elected local authority:

- 'within the family' organisations, i.e. organisations explicitly created by the local authority in response to fragmentation pressures, or specifically selected by the local authority to provide services (e.g. local authority created development companies)

- traditionally free-standing organisations, i.e. organisations which have not, within the experience of councillors and local authority officers, been created to take over local government functions (e.g. parts of the health service)

- domain intruders, i.e. organisations which have been created in recent years and which have taken functions away from local government (e.g. Urban Development Corporations, grant maintained schools, etc.).

Work by Painter *et al.* (1996), also for the LGMB, complements the above work and seeks to identify examples of good practice in responding to fragmentation. All the aforementioned projects are based on a mix of interview and desk-based research.

Skelcher and Davis (1995) identified three key issues for attention:

- the consequences for public accountability

- maintaining (or recreating) the ability to respond to issues requiring co-ordinated action from a number of functions or services

- the appropriateness and adequacy of existing democratic mechanisms and processes which have been so easily undermined in recent years.

These are reflected in the dilemmas facing local authorities. On the one hand, as the elected voice of their communities, they have a legitimate concern about the nature, quality and impact of services provided by local hospitals, local grant maintained schools, and other QUANGOs. On the other hand, in the interests of the local community, local authorities have to work with these bodies, because of the way in which their own direct responsibilities have been reduced; the consequential inter-agency nature of many public policy issues; and the severe, government-imposed, restrictions on local government finance. Partnership is a necessity but the roles of community voice and advocate on the one hand, and of partner on the other, are not always mutually compatible. Local authorities are therefore having to continually consider the issues raised by fragmentation. The second report of the Nolan Committee (Committee on Standards in Public Life, 1996) calls for pilot schemes 'involving local authorities and others' to increase the local accountability of non-elected bodies providing local public services.

QUANGOs in operation

QUANGOs are responsible for a wide range of public services, but in comparison with central and local government there is relatively little research on the way in which they behave in practice. What research there is covers three main areas – the internal operation of the organisation, relationships with other agencies and the public, and service performance. It also concentrates on local rather than national bodies. There are two factors that highlight the importance of research in this area. The first is the series of cases of financial mismanagement and poor governance by QUANGOs, including those investigated by the District Audit Service (Audit Commission, 1993), the Public Accounts Committee (House of Commons, 1994) and the Further Education Funding Council (Shattock, 1994). Secondly, the relative lack of openness on the part of many QUANGOs makes it a matter of public interest that their decision processes and performance should be scrutinised and relevant policy recommendations drawn.

Internal operation

Some types of QUANGO differ markedly from the local and central government convention that separates the roles of elected politicians and permanent officials. Health service bodies are the most stark example. Here there are normally five executives (i.e. senior managers), five non-executives and a non-executive chair. The balance is somewhat different on TEC and further education governing bodies, there normally being no more than one or two executive members compared with 15 to 20 non-executives. This elevation of paid officials to full member status raises questions about the balance of power in board meetings, especially when considered in terms of the concern to distinguish political and managerial roles in local and central government (e.g. Armstrong, 1985; Widdicombe Committee [Committee of Enquiry into the Conduct of Local Authority Business], 1986; House of Commons Treasury and Civil Service Select Committee, 1994).

In practice it appears that board meetings are largely collegial affairs with members, other than the chair, having equal status. In health service bodies, there is little distinction between the role of non-executives and executives in the decision process at board level. Since individuals who openly oppose the body or its policies are unlikely to be appointed, there is a potential for decisions to be reached without the close and critical scrutiny that arises in elected systems with a formalised 'loyal opposition' (Skelcher and Davis, 1995; Ferlie *et al.*, 1995). There was considerable variation in the extent to which non-executives in the eight types of local QUANGO surveyed by Skelcher and Davis felt they were 'rubber stamping' managers' recommendations. However, Ashburner (1993) found that executives had a major influence on the board agenda and that their recommendations were almost always carried. This could be an indication of the power of the executives. Alternatively it may be the outcome of a more subtle process by which proposals emerge from informal discussions and agreements with the chair and other non-executives and the board is merely ratifying these agreements. Some studies have gathered observational data on the nature and extent of non-executive involvement in board decision-making (Ferlie *et al.*, 1993; Ferlie *et al.*, 1996; Peck, 1995).

The operation of the board relates in part to members' motives and role perceptions. Studies of the pre-reorganisation health authorities posited that non-executives would either be *tribunes* who saw themselves as community representatives, *prefects* acting as the agent of higher tiers of government or *patriarchs* who were loyal to health staff (Ranade, 1985). Although this distinction appears to have been removed in the post-reorganisation health authorities and trusts, the question of how board members see their role remains. In the case of school governing bodies, which admittedly have some elected parent governors, it appears that they tend to support and advise the headteacher and staff rather than taking a more managerial role of ensuring the efficient and effective operation of the school (Levacic, 1995). Studies of TECs (Emmerich and Peck, 1992) and the new health service trusts (Ferlie *et al.*, 1993) conclude that non-executives see themselves dealing with questions that are amenable to technical solutions rather than political, value-based conflicts. However, recent cases of explicit rationing decisions being made by health authorities indicates that this conclusion may need revision. West and Sheaff (1994) have investigated the ethical codes board members apply and identify a degree of confusion.

Members' perceptions of their role will also be shaped because they are normally selected for appointment rather than individually deciding that they wish to join a particular board. In this way they differ from Members of Parliament and local councillors, despite Pettigrew *et al.*'s (1991) use of the term *elite volunteer*. However, the advertisement of Police Authority, and some health service, non-executive positions in England since 1994 marks the beginnings of a new pattern of recruitment.

Relationships with other agencies and the public

Public service bodies increasingly operate in an environment where they must interact with other agencies either to secure resources or deliver programmes. This is true of many QUANGOs, some of which already incorporate a number of different interests in their board structure. The different cultures of public, private and voluntary sectors affect the ability of these parties to work together as does the competitive environment. Consequently, there tends to be a degree of suspicion and mistrust (Thomas, 1994). The role of the board can be important in this context, taking a lead to build relationships with other organisations (Crowley-Bainton, 1993; Vaughan, 1993).

Relationships between QUANGOs and the public have not been the subject of a great deal of research. Painter *et al.* (1994) commented on the high degree of variability in the attitude and approaches used by different bodies. The lack of public involvement has long been noted on the part of some Urban Development Corporations (Imrie, 1993). Hall and Weir (1996) report on the openness, or otherwise, of a range of QUANGOs and on the application of the Citizen's Charter to such bodies.

The Channel 4/ICM survey (Dunleavy and Weir, 1994) explicitly investigated attitudes to the way in which public services were governed. This survey found that out of seven services subject to recent changes in governance structure, only in the case of the Police did respondents express a view in favour of appointed bodies. Greer and Hoggett (1995) review this research as well as the number and results of ballots for school transfer to grant-maintained status and the large-scale voluntary transfer of council housing to housing associations. They conclude that individuals may opt for a service to transfer to another organisation if it appears to have more resources, even if they are opposed in principle to the service being governed by an appointed or self-appointing body.

Service performance

The debate about the rights and wrongs of QUANGOs as a means of governing public services has rarely extended to an evaluation of their performance in the commissioning and delivery of services. House of Commons Select Committees, on the other hand, have been particularly interested in assessing the achievements of QUANGOs and the extent to which they are giving value for money. The area in which most performance-related research has been undertaken is urban regeneration, especially in relation to Urban Development Corporations and City Challenge. These studies conclude that the success of such bodies has been variable. They raise questions about the distributional impact of their policies and the relative exclusion of the community (e.g. Brownhill, 1990; Docklands Consultative Committee, 1992; Imrie, 1993).

The development of citizens' charters and the publication of explicit service standards has led to research into their impact on quality and performance. Beale and Pollitt (1994) assessed the operation of charters in a range of local authority and appointed services. Their conclusions are based on the nature and degree of professionalisation of the service rather than its governance structure, but this research provides a useful basis for comparative study.

Accountability

The accountability of QUANGOs has been the subject of considerable political debate in recent years. Much has been written on this question, but relatively little social science research has been conducted. One of the most important and detailed studies, that by Day and Klein (1987), is now quite dated in its empirical focus. The research includes analyses of the water and health authority sectors, one of which has been privatised while the other has been substantially reorganised. However, the research findings are still very relevant in drawing attention to the way in which board members perceive their accountability and investigating the manner in which this is exercised. Because they examined appointed and elected bodies, Day and Klein were also able to develop an analysis in terms of these two types of members. They argue, for example, that the view that elected members are accountable by virtue of election while appointed members are not, ignores questions about their respective ability to control the services for which they are responsible. They develop a more complex analysis in which the control of officials relates to members' capacity to be answerable for their services, and suggest that this cuts across the otherwise neat distinction between the two sectors. This is one of the few pieces of research that develops comparative analysis between elected and appointed members.

Accountability has been researched in other ways in recent years. Plummer's study of *The Governance Gap* concluded that the 'current arrangements for accountability are so confused and contradictory as to be probably unsustainable' (Plummer, 1994). Ashburner (1993) identified a perception by health authority and health trust non-executives that they had multiple accountability relationships. Members felt that the board as a whole had a strong accountability to the Secretary of State and also to the local community and patients. Returning to the Day and Klein work, the question remains as to how those accountability relationships operate in practice. There is, in fact, a discrepancy between members' feelings of accountability to the local community and the processes by which members relate to that community (Skelcher and Davis, 1995). This is accentuated by ambiguities and uncertainties in the accountability framework of local appointed bodies, often related to their membership structure and operational context. For example, Training and Enterprise Councils have seats on the board reserved for the voluntary sector, local authority and trade unions. However, because TECs are registered under companies legislation, these directors must act as individuals making decisions in the best interests of the company rather than as representatives of their particular sector. As we noted earlier, this raises the question of how these dual roles are managed in practice.

Weir (1995) broadens the discussion of accountability by examining the formal accountability mechanisms and safeguards applying across the national and local appointed sector. He concludes that they are inconsistent and ineffective and argues in favour of wider constitutional reforms. At a more local level Painter *et al.* (1994) draw similar conclusions from their study of the West Midlands. This analysis of accountability should be seen in the context of a growing public service consumerism. The limited accountability of QUANGOs to the community as a whole, especially in the case of those boards that formerly had local authority representation as of right, has occurred at the same time as individual users are presented with charters and service standards. The interests of the user now come above the rights of citizens to hold public or publicly-funded bodies to account (Payne, 1994).

The general debate on accountability has led to the publication of various pieces of guidance for QUANGOs. Examples include the TEC National Council's Local Accountability Framework (1995) and the 1994 Codes of Conduct and Accountability for the Health Service. This guidance seeks to strengthen the accountability of non-executives and chairs but, in a context where commercial pressures are strong, informal processes have developed and boards value their autonomy – which in the case of health service trusts, further education colleges and others is new found.

Conclusions and reflection

The debate about QUANGOs is unlikely to end in the foreseeable future. There are too many questions about this method of delivering public services, especially local public services, for the issue to disappear rapidly. Even if there is a change of government the present indications are that most, if not all, of the current questions will remain relevant.

In the preceding pages we have sought to pick out key themes in the debate. It is hard to escape the conclusion that, taken in the round, the combined effect of the growth of QUANGOs and the more general reforms to the management of public services – the 'new management' – has been to centralise decision-making on key aspects of many of our public services.

This brings with it potential problems of overload for central government as ultimate decider and arbiter on an ever-increasing range of issues. In addition, the increasing fragmentation of responsibilities for individual services in any given community is not replaced by compensating integration at either local or national level. Central government, particularly in England, is largely made up of a federation of relatively autonomous ministries and departments which are only loosely brought together through Cabinet mechanisms. (The new Government Offices in the English regions provide a limited degree of integration but this is largely in relation to the processing of urban regeneration funding.)

For much of the period since the Second World War there was a subtle mixture of national and local democratic inputs to services. For example, a 'centrally determined, locally administered' school system symbolised a balance between the 'vertical' integration required by central government in a national education system, and local 'horizontal' integration with the network of other services which bear on the effectiveness of education services.

QUANGOisation has led to increased 'vertical' integration, with performance targets for services intended to increase efficiency. But this 'vertical' integration has largely been in functional 'chimneys' unable to easily respond across the organisational divide. For example, in bodies such as health authorities and health service trusts the 'vertical' linkages to the NHS Executive and Department of Health may take precedence over the necessary 'horizontal' linkages. Yet, as Stewart and Davis (1994) note:

many of the emerging issues in our society require … a capacity for integration. The environmental issue and the aspiration to sustainable development, the growth of crime and the aspiration to safer communities, racial discrimination and the aspiration to equal opportunities, are all issues which require different organisations and institutions to work together. They cannot be resolved on a functional basis.

Democratic processes legitimise public policy. QUANGOs may well have been intended to increase efficiency and effectiveness. They may indeed have achieved this in certain circumstances. But this has been at the expense of the ability of elected local government to provide civic leadership and integration.

This is a rapidly developing field with much potential for further research. Three main themes suggest themselves. The first concerns the experience of being an appointed member and the nature of the roles that such individuals play both on and off the board. We know little about the realities of life as a board member, especially on national quangos, nor the issues that they face. This might assist understanding of links between members and any political party structures. Secondly, research could explore the question of fragmentation and the problems of developing the capacity to respond to issues requiring co-ordinated action from a number of bodies, especially where these have different governmental structures and cultures. Of particular importance here is the impact of integrating mechanisms on the accountabilities and responsibilities of elected bodies. A third research agenda is the development of comparative studies within the appointed sector. The sector is often discussed as if it were a uniform set of institutions. There are, however, considerable differences between types of QUANGO, and the implications of such variety – for example in terms of public involvement and members' roles – would aid both understanding of this sector and the development of policy recommendations for corporate governance.

Appendix: An analysis of selected research into QUANGOs

Here we provide an analysis of the key features of selected recent research into QUANGOs.

Author	Focus	Method	Comments
Ashburner, 1993; Ashburner and Cairncross, 1993; Ferlie, Ashburner and Fitzgerald, 1993; etc.	Board members, executive and non-executive, of NHS Trusts and DHAs	National survey of all health authority members, semi-structured interviews and analysis of documents	Over 60% response rate for survey; large number of interviews and observations of boards at work. Due to timing, only covers first wave of NHS trusts whose chairs and non-executives were more likely to be active supporters of Government policy
Bastin, 1990	The composition of Higher Education Corporation governing bodies	Postal survey of all HE Corporations (polytechnics and major colleges)	73% response rate; presents picture immediately following incorporation. Lack of case study or interview data limits interpretation of results

BBC, 1994a	Register of members of non-departmental public bodies	Original data obtained from Parliamentary Questions	Comprehensive data source which has been little used; liable to become outdated; requires other name-based data sets to enable links to be made; likely to involve considerable investment for limited return – area studies probably more useful in building biographical profiles of QUANGO members
Beale and Pollitt, 1994	Assessment of charters in different public services	Interviews with users and staff in a housing department, schools, a hospital, GP practices and a local authority highways/environment dept	Considers the performance of different public services; enables comparison across elected and non-elected sectors
Crowley-Bainton, 1993	Relationships between TECs and employers	Qualitative study of six TECs, selected on the basis of travel-to-work area characteristics, involving interviews with TEC directors and managers and local employers and analysis of documents	Highlights factors affecting relationships between TECs and local employers; complements Vaughan survey
Davis, 1993	Local QUANGOs in the West Midlands	Use of published data to construct biographical profiles of non-executive members	Application of Davis and Stewart to one area

(Appendix cont'd)

Davis and Stewart, 1993	Governance and accountability structures of local non-elected bodies in England	Analysis of government and other documents	Mapping of formal features of these bodies
Day and Klein, 1987	Accountability in five public services	Study of water, health, police, social services and education boards/ committees; semi-structured interviews in some bodies, postal questionnaire in others	Detailed analysis of accountability within and between five types of public bodies – some elected, some appointed and some hybrids
Dunleavy and Weir, 1994	Survey of public attitudes to governance structures	ICM interviewed controlled quota sample of 1,427 adults in 103 constituencies	Reveals public preferences for the type of bodies that should be responsible for different public services
Greer and Hoggett, 1995	Non-elected bodies and local governance	Synthesis of available information on non-elected bodies using secondary sources	Detailed review of available information
Hall and Weir, 1995	National executive QUANGOs	Synthesis of a variety of published and other data on 10 bodies	Commentary and membership details, including brief biographies of some members
Hall and Weir, 1996	Executive and advisory QUANGOs	Uses official data and Parliamentary Answers	Reviews the openness to the public of QUANGOs responsible to various government ministries

Levacic, 1995	Role of school governing bodies	Interviews and observation of 11 governing bodies of schools serving communities with different socio-economic characteristics	In-depth tracking of governing bodies
Morgan and Roberts, 1993	Guide to QUANGOs in Wales	Data largely obtained from government, Parliamentary and other published sources	
Painter, Isaac-Henry and Chalcroft, 1994	Assessment of accountability, member recruitment and public participation in local QUANGOs in the West Midlands	Interviews with non-executives and executives from QUANGOs in the health, urban regeneration, housing, training and education fields	
Payne, 1994	Accountability and accessibility of local QUANGOs in Basildon, Essex	Survey of local QUANGOs in one locality and construction of accountability and accessibility index	Small-scale case study
Peck, 1995	Operation of NHS Trust board	Interviews, analysis of minutes and observation of one board	In-depth study of one board
Peck, 1993	Assessment of TEC initiative	Case studies of four TECs together with review of national training developments	Illustrates difficulties in applying national policy on this new type of body

(Appendix cont'd)

Ranade, 1985	Role of health authority members	Semi-structured interviews, repertory grid, diary keeping, observation of meetings and review of documents in 10 district health authorities	Pre-dates reorganisation of district health authorities and introduction of NHS Trusts
Robinson and Shaw, 1994	Membership of local QUANGOs in the North-East of England	Use of published data and other sources to construct biographical profiles of non-executive members	
Skelcher and Davis, 1995	Characteristics and attitudes of non-executive members of local appointed bodies	Postal questionnaire of non-executives, covering City Challenge, UDCs, HATs, FE Colleges, TECs, Careers Pathfinders, DHAs and NHS Trusts, supplemented with semi-structured interviews	First large-scale survey of members across the local appointed sector; response rate (37%) and number of questionnaires returned (1,508) satisfactory for analysis and interpretation. Identifies differences between sectors
Skelcher and Stewart, 1993	Local QUANGOs in London	Assessment of secondary data; construction of accountability index	

Thomas, 1994	Relationships between local authorities and TECs	Survey of all metropolitan district councils and London borough councils	63% response rate; good overview of local authority attitudes to TECs and assessment of linkages through board membership and other devices. Does not consider the relationship from the TECs' point of view
Vaughan, 1993	Relationships between TECs and employers	Postal survey of all TEC chief executives together with analysis of data held by the Department of Employment	Overview of TEC formal relationships
Weir and Hall (eds), 1994	Extra-governmental organisations at local, regional and national levels	Assessment using published sources and data obtained via Parliamentary Questions	Comprehensive data on numbers of members and expenditure of bodies; tabulates accountability and probity features; family trees of departmental sponsorship of QUANGOs
West and Sheaff, 1994	Ethical issues facing NHS members	Postal questionnaire containing 53 items on a five point scale	52% response rate; could be supplemented by interviews or case studies to illustrate how these ethical dilemmas are resolved

References

Armstrong, R. (1985) 'Ministers, politicians and civil servants', *Public Money*, September

Ashburner, L. (1993) 'The composition of NHS Trust Boards', in E. Peck and P. Spurgeon, *NHS Trusts in Practice*. Longman

Ashburner, L. and Cairncross, L. (1993) 'Membership of the new style Health Authorities', *Public Administration*, vol. 71

Audit Commission (1993) *Adding Up the Sums: The Management of School Finances*. HMSO

Bastin, N. (1990) 'The composition of governing bodies of Higher Education Corporations', *Higher Education Quarterly*, vol. 44

BBC (1994a) *Here and Now QUANGO Directory*. BBC Political Research Unit

BBC (1994b), 'Tory Party donors get top QUANGO jobs', BBC News Release, 28 November

BBC (1994c), 'QUANGO king works eight days a week', BBC News Release, 20 December

Beale, V. and Pollitt, C. (1994) 'Charters at the grass roots', *Local Government Studies*, vol. 20

Brownhill, S. (1990) *Developing London's Docklands: Another Great Planning Disaster?* Paul Chapman Publishing

Cabinet Office (annually) *Public Bodies*, HMSO

Colenutt, B. and Ellis, G. (1993) 'The next QUANGOs in London', *New Statesman and Society*, 26 March

Committee of Enquiry into the Conduct of Local Authority Business (The Widdicombe Committee) (1986) *Report*, Cmnd 9798. HMSO

Committee on Standards in Public Life (The Nolan Committee) (1995) *First Report*, Cmnd 2850-I and Cmnd 2850-II. HMSO, May

Committee on Standards in Public Life (The Nolan Committee) (1995b) *Local Public Spending Bodies: Issues and Questions*. HMSO, August

Committee on Standards in Public Life (The Nolan Committee) (1996) *Second Report: Local Public Spending Bodies*, Cmnd 3270-I and Cmnd 3270-II. HMSO, May

Crowley-Bainton, T. (1993) *TECs and Employers: Developing Effective Links: Part 2*. Department of Employment

Davis, H. (1993) *A First Guide to Appointed Local Executive Bodies in the West Midlands*. INLOGOV and Birmingham City Council, December

Davis, H. (1994) *Appointed Local Bodies in the West Midlands*. INLOGOV

Davis, H. and Daly, G. (1995) 'Codes of conduct are not enough', *The IHSM Network*, vol. 2, no. 4

Davis, H. and Spencer, K. (1995) *Housing Associations and the Governance Debate*. School of Public Policy, The University of Birmingham, March

Davis, H. and Stewart, J. (1993) *The Growth of Government by Appointment: Implications for Local Democracy*. Local Government Management Board, September

Day, P. and Klein, R. (1987) *Accountabilities in Five Public Services*. Tavistock Publications

Docklands Consultative Committee (1992) *All That Glitters is Not Gold: A Critical Assessment of Canary Wharf*. London

Doig, A. (1977) 'Public bodies and ministerial patronage', *Parliamentary Affairs*, Winter

Dunleavy, P. and Weir, S. (1994) 'Democracy in doubt', *Local Government Chronicle*, 29 April

Emmerich, M. and Peck, J. (1992) *Reforming the TECs*. CLES

Ferlie, E., Ashburner, L. and Fitzgerald, L. (1993) 'Movers and shakers', *Health Service Journal*, 18 November

Ferlie, E., Ashburner, L. and Fitzgerald, L. (1995) 'Corporate governance and the public sector: some issues and evidence from the NHS', *Public Administration*, vol. 73, Autumn

Ferlie, E., Fitzgerald, L. and Ashburner, L. (1996) 'Corporate governance in the post 1990 NHS: the role of the board', *Public Money and Management*, April-June

Grayson, L. and Davis, H. (1996) *INLOGOV Informs on QUANGOs*. INLOGOV

Graystone, J. (1991) *New Governing Bodies in Maintained FE: Size and Composition*. The Staff College

Greer, A. and Hoggett, P. (1995) 'Non-elected bodies and local governance', in *The QUANGO State: An Alternative Approach*.. Commission for Local Democracy, February

Hall, W. and Weir, S. (1995) ' National executive QUANGOs', in *Briefing Papers for the Nolan Committee*. INLOGOV

Hall, W. and Weir, S. (1996) *The Untouchables: Power and Accountability in the QUANGO State*. The Scarman Trust

House of Commons Committee of Public Accounts (1994) *Eighth Report: The Proper Conduct of Public Business*. January

House of Commons Treasury and Civil Service Select Committee (1994) *The Role of the Civil Service*, vol. 1, HC27

Imrie, R. (1993) *British Urban Policy and the Urban Development Corporations*. Paul Chapman Publishing

Klein, R. and Day, P. (undated) *Building on Success: Improving Housing Association Governance*. Southern Housing Group

Labour Research Department (1994) *Who Runs Our Health Service?* GMB, October

Leach, S., Clarke, M., Campbell, A., Davis, H. and Rogers, S. (1996) *Minimising Fragmentation: Managing Services: Leading Communities*. Local Government Management Board

Levacic, R. (1995) 'School governing bodies: management boards or supporters clubs?', *Public Money and Management*, April-June

Loveday, B. (1995) 'Who are the independent members on the new Police Authorities?', *County News*, Association of County Councils, April

MacFarlane, R. (1993) *Community Involvement in City Challenge*. NCVO

Midwinter, A. (1995) 'QUANGOs in Scotland', in *Briefing Papers for the Nolan Committee*. INLOGOV

Morgan, K. and Osmond, J. (1995) 'The Welsh QUANGO State', in *Briefing Papers for the Nolan Committee*. INLOGOV

Morgan, K. and Roberts, E. (1993) *The Democratic Deficit: A Guide to QUANGOland*. University of Wales, October

Painter, C., Isaac-Henry, K. and Chalcroft, T. (1994) *Appointed Agencies and Public Accountability: Proactive Strategies for Local Government*. West Midlands Joint Committee, August

Painter, C., Rouse, J., Isaac-Henry, K. and Munk, L. (1996) *Changing Local Governance: Local Authorities and Non-elected Agencies*. Local Government Management Board

Payne, T. (1994) *The Accountability and Accessibility of Locally Appointed Executive Agencies*. MA Thesis, University of Essex

Peck, E. (1995) 'The performance of an NHS trust board: actors' accounts, minutes and observation', *British Journal of Management*, vol. 6

Peck, J. (1993) 'The trouble with TECs', *Policy and Politics*, vol. 21, no. 4

Pettigrew, A. *et al.* (1991) 'The leadership role of the new Health Authorities', *Public Money and Management*, Spring

Plummer, J. (1994) *The Governance Gap: QUANGOs and Accountability*. LGC Communications and Joseph Rowntree Foundation

Ranade, W. (1985) 'Motives and behaviour in District Health Authorities', *Public Administration*, vol. 63

Robinson, F. and Shaw, K. (1994) *Who Runs the North?* UNISON, November

Shattock, M. (1994) *Derby College, Wilmorton.* Further Education Funding Council, November

Skelcher, C. and Davis, H. (1995) *Opening the Boardroom Door: Membership of Local Appointed Bodies.* LGC Communications and Joseph Rowntree Foundation

Skelcher, C. and Stewart, J. (1993) *The Appointed Government of London.* Association of London Authorities

Stewart, J. and Davis, H. (1994) 'A new agenda for local governance', *Public Money and Management*, vol. 14, no. 4

TEC National Council (1995) *A Framework for the Local Accountability of Training and Enterprise Councils in England and Wales*, July

Thomas, I. (1994) 'The relationship between local authorities and TECs in metropolitan areas', *Local Government Studies*, vol. 20

Vaughan, P. (1993) *TECs and Employers: Developing Effective Links: Part 1.* Department of Employment

Weir, S. (1995) 'Questions of democratic accountability', *Parliamentary Affairs*, vol. 48

Weir, S. and Hall, W. (1994) (eds) *EGO Trip: Extra-Governmental Organisations in the United Kingdom and their Accountability.* Charter 88 Trust, May

West, M. and Sheaff, R. (1994) 'Back to basics', *Health Service Journal*, vol. 24 November

Wright, T. (1995) 'Beyond the patronage state', Fabian Society pamphlet 569, February

2 Local government and the new public management: A review

Michael Clarke

We in the ages lying
In the buried past of the earth,
Built Nineveh with our sighing,
And Babel itself in our imerth;
And o'erthrew them with prophesying
To the old of the new world's worth;
For each age is a dream that is dying,
Or one that is coming to birth

(Arthur O'Shaughnessey,
1844–81)

Introduction

As part of the final stage of its work, the Joseph Rowntree Foundation's Local and Central Government Relations Research Committee has commissioned a number of synthesis papers to bring together research findings in a number of key areas of interest. The Committee's intention is that these papers should draw on its own research programme and on the parallel research programmes of a number of other organisations – particularly the Economic and Social Research Council (principally through its Local Governance Programme), the Commission for Local Democracy, the Local Government Management Board, the Department of the Environment and the Audit Commission.

Among the themes selected by the Committee is the 'new public sector management' and that is the focus for this paper. The Committee's brief asks that the paper:

- review the relevant published and ongoing research

- evaluate consistency and coherence in research findings

- identify and interpret key themes arising from the research

- consider the implications for:

  - local government powers, roles, structures

  - local and central government relations

- identify the key questions which the research leaves unanswered

- reflect on the lessons from the research for current and future policies relating to local government.

Inevitably, the importance of these categories will vary between the various synthesis papers. For the sake of clarity and ease of reference the categories will be used in the presentation of this paper.

The new public management

There is a need, to start with, to understand what is meant by the new public management and how it is to be defined in relation to local government. This is important for two reasons. First because, although there is no coherently organised programme of research which focuses on the subject, there are plenty of references to it – but often in an ill-defined way. The second is because of the way the label is sometimes used to imply a coherent, intellectually consistent and well-understood model or approach to management, and sometimes only to capture a trend or set of new emphases.

Much of the general literature on the new public management is about the public sector generally (rather than local government specifically) and much of it is international rather than specifically British (even if Anglo-Saxon and Anglo-American influence is predominant). From the turn of this decade, a series of writings began to appear, drawing on the public management reform programme of the 1980s (seen most obviously in Britain, the USA, New Zealand, Australia and Canada but spreading more widely, not least under the influence of the World Bank, the IMF and other international agencies, to the developing world) and suggesting the emergence of a new model or paradigm (e.g. Aucoin, 1993; Hood, 1991; Osborne and Gaebler, 1992; Ingraham and Romzek, 1993).

The distinctive elements of the new model were variously defined. To capture the essence, three examples will suffice. First Hood (1991), who identified seven components of the new public management:

- 'hands-on' professional management in the public sector

- explicit standards and measures of performance

- greater emphasis on output controls

- disaggregation of organisational units in the public sector

- greater competition in the public sector

- stress on private-sector styles of management practice

- stress on greater discipline and parsimony in resource use.

Two years later, Walsh and Stewart (1992) identified the development of a new public management in (particularly sub-national) government in Britain characterised by:

- the separation of purchaser and provider

- the growth of contracts

- accountability for performance

- flexibility of pay and conditions

- the separation of political process from management process

- the creation of markets and quasi-markets

- the public as customers

- the regulatory role of government

- a change of culture.

In the same year, Osborne and Gaebler (1992) published what has, in many ways, become a key source-book and reference point for the new public management. They addressed the 're-invention' of government in the USA (primarily at state and local level) around ten core themes:

- catalytic government, steering rather than rowing

- community-owned government, empowering rather than serving

- competitive government, injecting competition into service delivery

- mission-driven government in place of rule-driven government

- results-oriented government, funding outcomes not inputs

- customer-driven government, meeting customer needs not bureaucracy

- enterprising government, earning rather than spending

- anticipatory government, focusing on prevention rather than cure

- decentralised government, shifting from hierarchy to participation and team work

- market-oriented government, leveraging change through the market.

In common with other authors, they argue the arrival of the new 'paradigm', borrowing from Kuhn (1970) the idea of a scientific paradigm as 'a set of assumptions about reality – an accepted model or pattern – that explained the world better than any other set of assumptions … [which] as long as it is explained most observed phenomena and solved the problems most people wanted solved, remained dominant'.

While this is not the place to debate this at any length, two sets of questions arise. First, is there a distinctive, consistent, complete and new set of assumptions about reality which is widely shared and understood? And, second, if there is a 'new paradigm' presumably there was an 'old' paradigm against which it can be set and evaluated?

On the first question, there undoubtedly are some common intellectual antecedents which might imply the basis for a new paradigm – public choice theory, neo-liberal ideas and the thinking of the new right. However, the fact of variety in the way the new public management is defined and the inclusion of characteristics whose origins are very different (e.g. customer focus derived from the service management revolution of the mid-1980s and the Peters and Waterman (1984) school of management thought) and apparent inconsistency between some of the elements (e.g. the 'harder' edge of management with emphasis on performance and outcomes and the 'softer' concerns of people, culture and so on) suggests caution. Having played his part in encouraging the idea of a model or paradigm, Hood (1995) now points to the fact that, while common labels (and jargon) may be being used, the actual content of what is being done in different places varies widely.

On the second point, the issue is far from the simplicity implied by Osborne and Gaebler (1992). It may be easy to define 'old style' characteristics and compare them with 'new' ones – and there has undoubtedly been a shift from emphasis on public 'administration' to public 'management' during the last couple of decades. But that is not necessarily the same thing as defining a movement from one paradigm to another. The old public administration shifted in its definition and description over time, and the debate of the seventies and the eighties which captured the shift from administration to management, while identifying the significance of the difference, did not try to argue a coherence and consistency which would be implied by the idea of a paradigm. Many of the elements of public management as defined in that period live on in the 'new public management', while others have gone and new elements (notably the market and competition and their consequences) have arrived.

All of this suggests a rather less colourful or more mundane possibility. Rather than the shift between paradigms, we may be seeing no more than a change of emphasis and focus in management – another stage in the evolution of ideas and practice. This would fit the argument that we do not actually know how best to administer or manage the business of government and that the history of the last century – let alone the last few decades – has been about the continual search for solutions to meet new circumstances.

If this is the case, we could go on to say that over the decades, while particular sets of assumptions, trends and fashions may have been apparent, there has been a consistently shifting ground – and continuous experiment with, and espousal, of new ideas and possibilities. Some of these may derive from bodies of theory and 'whole world' views; others may just be the practical attempts to learn and adapt from practice and changing circumstances.

Post hoc rationalisation and/or the academic construction of theories and frameworks to explain (or, more probably, describe) what seems to 'be' at any point in time may be fun, but may obscure a more ordinary reality. It is interesting to note that some of the more thoughtful commentaries on the American public management 'revolution' and the pursuit of the new paradigm

Dilulio *et al.*, 1994; Kettl and Dilulio, 1995) made the point that *evolution* of approach and practice through a continuum of ideas and experience is a more realistic picture than the replacement of one paradigm by another. This is echoed by Walsh (1995) in his analysis of market and competitive mechanisms with its implication that there are both more and less good/successful consequences and that as time and experience progress, so form and content will be likely to change. Gray and Jenkins (1995) and Clarke (1996) also adduce arguments about the nature of change, about evolution, experiment and continuing renewal rather than revolution, re-invention and, more abstractly, shifts between paradigms.

One more general point about this debate, to which we shall return later. Notwithstanding the attempts to construct theory and to advance intellectual argument about changes in management, much of the new public management literature is based on assertion rather than a solid empirical base. Hood and Jackson (1991) draw attention to the importance and role of assertion in the development of thinking about administration and management. Suffice it to say that there is a streak of almost evangelistic fervour about many of the ideas and strands associated with the new public management; some of this has an ideological base and some of it appears to have more to do with 'good' or 'right' ideas.

Where does all of this take us? First, there is sufficient reason to doubt the claims of a paradigm shift and the emergence of an intellectually coherent, internally consistent and commonly understood framework which defines a 'new' public management as opposed to something else which had gone before. Secondly, however, as the Hood (1990), Stewart and Walsh (1992) and Osborne and Gaebler (1992) examples testify, there are certainly new emphases and trends at work (i.e. focus on performance, disaggregation, empowerment) and new approaches being introduced (i.e. competition and markets). Thirdly, the espousal of the new ideas and emphases is widespread – as may have been some of their predecessors for that matter – and acceptance is common.

Taking all of this together, therefore, it may be more helpful to think in terms of predominant, but ever-changing, orthodoxies rather than of paradigms or single models. In the light of this, coherence, consistency, shared understanding and definition become less important than they would otherwise be. 'New public management' then comes to have less claim as an abstract construct than as the definition of broad and discernible strands which characterise the current orthodoxies and fashions of management.

In reviewing recent and current research – and identifying ideas for new work – this paper will be looking for any light which research sheds on the elements of the new orthodoxy and its consequences.

The research

Programmes, funders and subjects

The point has already been made that the new public management has not been the central focus for any major programme of research. Rather, elements of it have caught the attention of a wide range of individual projects – sometimes more or less incidentally, sometimes as a central theme.

The major programmes of local government research funded by the Joseph Rowntree Foundation and the ESRC have cast their attentions across a wide canvas, albeit with particular interests in central–local relations and the emerging pattern of local governance respectively. The Commission for Local Democracy funded a range of synthesis and ideas papers, drawing on research undertaken for other purposes. Its work was more concerned with the enhancement of local democracy and the structures and processes supporting it than with management per se. The Local Government Management Board commissions work to elicit better understanding of particular management issues and developing practice – largely to underpin its own work of promoting better management. The Department of the Environment also commissions carefully targeted work, some of which has a policy-related or management focus (notably on competition in recent years). The Audit Commission's primary interest is to describe and review current and emerging management practice, both to promote improvement and to underpin its audit work.

As a way of exploring what the research has to say about the new public management, a series of themes which exemplify the characteristics of the definitions outlined at the beginning of the last section will be used. These are:

• competition, contracts and markets

• disaggregation, fragmentation and integration

• empowerment

• performance and quality

• change management

- professionalism of management

- steering not rowing.

In each case key themes and findings will be identified and described. In the section which follows we will go on to assess consistency and coherence.

Research themes

Competition, contracts and markets

Competition (especially CCT), the development of markets or quasi-markets (i.e. le Grand and Bartlett, 1993) and the emergence of a contract culture have often been taken as the cornerstone of a new public management. Many observers and practitioners have drawn attention to the impact of CCT on the internal operations of the local authority, on styles of management, on the way in which managers behave and to the beneficial impact it has had on service delivery. There is little hard evidence which compares the new with old patterns of service delivery, but there is a lot of material which explores the new patterns and assesses some of the impact. Broadly similar conclusions emerge from the various pieces of work.

The first LGMB organisational change survey (*LGMB*: Young, 1993) provided useful evidence of the impact on organisation and management. The survey was launched as the first of a time-series with the intention to report every two years. The results of the 1994 survey (*LGMB*: 1996) take the story further. The 1992 survey revealed a series of positive views from chief executives about the impact of CCT on the organisation in general, on culture and on management processes. Two years later the second survey suggested more caution on these themes but a much clearer view about the effects CCT has had on general attitudes and approaches to service delivery. Despite the caution about organisational and cultural impact, the 1994 results show that changes in the way central support services are provided and the development of internal 'markets' have gone on apace. (The move towards CCT for white-collar and professional services is likely to maintain this momentum and will be monitored closely. The DoE has commissioned research to match that conducted by Walsh and Davis (*DoE*: 1993) for manual services).

The LGMB surveys confirm the pattern of client/contractor separation urged by the Audit Commission and others. In 1992, 74 per cent of authorities indicated no split in housing (one of the two services tracked) whereas two years later the figure was 7 per cent (social services represented a service further ahead – not least under the impact of the community care legislation – and showed 'no split' figures of 8 per cent and 7 per cent respectively).

The impact on management, culture and organisational process is important. The LGMB 1994 results suggested further probing may be necessary. Other research evidence is nearer to the 1992 conclusions. Rao and Young (*Rowntree*: 1995) appear to confirm a significant impact and one which is welcomed. The beneficial effects on delivery of service (customer-driven, with requirements being made explicit and satisfaction taken seriously) are shown to have been a major influence inside the organisation. From their evidence, the authors conclude that the realities of competition will remain even if a future government were to remove the element of compulsion – 'the dynamics of competition have proved powerful beyond all expectation ... Britain is unlikely to see the old patterns of public service management again.' Managers are shown to have let go of long-established attitudes and practices.

Rao and Young (1995) also draw attention to the constraints of nationally determined pay and conditions of service and to the loss of jobs and cuts in pay and conditions which have been necessary for productivity gains in the successfully competitive authorities. They also note variety, from place to place, in the intensity of competition. These conclusions confirm the findings of the more extensive monitoring research commissioned by the DoE (Walsh and Davis (*DoE*: 1993) and Walker (*DoE*: 1993)). Both show the significant impact on management, the extent of the client/contractor split, the impact on pay and conditions and the changes in support services – with the development of an internal market and significant decentralisation of responsibility to the managers of DLOs and DSOs. Walsh and Davis trace the extent of the effects on management and present a balance sheet of gains and disadvantages. Among the latter is the relatively little time the client spends on policy and service development and a suggestion (echoed more strongly by Rao and Young) that CCT produces sufficient fragmentation to stretch almost to breaking point the ability of any local authority to secure overall strategic direction.

Both DoE research commissions explore the consequences for political management, but only in structural terms. Both show more attention to the contractor side of the organisation with the creation of DSO and DLO committees and boards – the latter being smaller than conventional member committees and having more powers. Rao and Young (*Rowntree*: 1995), with evidence two years newer, show an enhancement of officer power at the expense of members, with the latter often feeling perplexed and marginalised in what they see to be an alien environment. This appears to confirm a widespread view, supported by anecdotal evidence, that elected members have been left behind in a programme of management change led by officers responding to externally driven requirements.

Two further research projects were commissioned by the DoE (underlining the political importance of CCT as a driver of change) – Ernst and Young (*DoE*: 1995) and BMRB (*DoE*: 1995). Both are about the external market and its extension. The former shows small firms absent because of the scale of most contracts. The latter explored private sector attitudes and reports an even split between those thinking they were discriminated against in some way or another and those believing private contractors to be favoured. For the first group, particular dissatisfaction comes from concern about local government's attitudes, processes and perceived lack of interest in quality. Interestingly, Rao and Young note that there is increasing concern for quality and a belief that this is likely to be central to the next stage of competition despite having been discouraged to date by tight regulation and an emphasis on price.

These various strands are drawn together in Walsh's *Public Service and Market Mechanisms*, published around the time of his death in 1995. This book draws on a wide understanding of practice, the literature of theory and ideas and research in local government and other parts of the public sector, and stands as a landmark text. Walsh spells out the benefits and disbenefits which have flowed from competition and contracting and underlines the extent to which market mechanisms have evolved and are continuing to change – indicating some key areas where further development is necessary. Among his themes is the importance of informal relationships between client and contractor and the development of trust – not least to allow for flexibility, adaptability and learning. The nature of contracts which can provide for this (see also Kay, 1994), is an important subject for future work.

The evolutionary nature of the development of markets and their application is also a central theme of Walsh and Stewart (*LGMB*: 1995). They point to the way in which public service markets are changing rapidly in their early stages of development and go on to raise important questions about the balance between the demands of markets on the one hand and political decisions about collective choice and provision on the other; they also pose the question of how far marketisation can be accommodated in the public service without the latter changing its nature beyond recognition. That, presumably, would be the point where an evolving trend or orthodoxy would become a new paradigm!

Disaggregation, fragmentation and integration

Competition and markets are seen to have contributed to fragmentation within local government – an aspect of the disaggregation of large bureaucratic organisations and the encouragement or creation of more closely focused organisations – which is seen as central to the new public management orthodoxy. A significant number of recent research contributions shed light both on these processes (and their reverse, the processes of integration) and on the performance of newly disaggregated organisations. Again, the studies capture emerging patterns and situations – even though the phenomena themselves are not new. Fragmentation, as the sense of internal differentiation, is a feature of most large or complex organisations; and the existence of separate organisations, with specific functions and existing alongside the local authority, have long been a feature of government and public provision in the local community.

The greatest attention has been given to the growth of local QUANGOs and their role and status as part of the system of local governance. The preceding paper to this on local QUANGOs has been prepared by Skelcher and Davis as part of the Local and Central Government Relations Committee's work. Suffice it to say that one recent piece of LGMB-commissioned research by Painter *et al.* (*LGMB*: 1996) has specifically explored the relationship between local authorities and local non-elected bodies. It looked at the situation in a sample of authorities and confirmed much of the conventional wisdom (e.g. that they had a negative effect on co-ordinated local service delivery but were willing collaborators; that they had served to weaken accountability but were capable of being monitored by local authorities – even if there was little consensus about good practice and few involved in actually tracking them; etc.). The research report provides checklists to prompt local authority action and warns of the problems of conflicting objectives when a local government seeks to monitor and review and be the advocate of local interests.

The negative aspects of disaggregation or fragmentation (in terms of weakening local government and service delivery, making difficulties for co-ordination and planning, blurring lines of accountability, etc.) are easy to argue. A local government which has seen itself being undermined has not been slow to do this. Some of the research has both reflected and encouraged this, lending support to assertion based on anecdote, ideology or defensiveness. Alexander (*LGMB*: 1993) caught this negative mood in his work on the management of fragmentation. Significantly, follow-up work commissioned by LGMB from Leach, Clarke *et al.* (*LGMB*: 1996) portrays a different picture. This work recognised that differentiation was a characteristic of any large or complex organisation or society and that managing such differentiation is a key task. Such management (of internal or external differentiation) is about finding ways of integrating. 'Fragmentation' (potentially a negative concept) was argued only to exist where there is differentiation without integration. The research explored the variety of means of integration available and revealed a positive view among managers and members that the challenge opened up new ways of working and opportunities.

Further testing of this will help. Parkinson *et al.* (*LGMB*: 1994) examines one important aspect of this in relationship to partnerships and urban regeneration. His work echoes other studies (notably evaluation research for DoE) in identifying the importance of partnership in post-1991 urban policy and the extent to which partnership is better than the conflictual and confrontational relationships which have characterised other chapters of urban policy. While not about special-purpose organisations as such, there is implicit endorsement of their contribution and potential in a context where collaboration and partnership can then serve to integrate. New skills and competences and structures and processes are needed; these deserve further examination.

Other research confirms the importance of partnerships as integrating mechanisms and, indeed, the importance of integration itself. Alcock, Craig *et al.* (*LGMB*: 1995), examining anti-poverty strategies, draw attention to the importance of cross-cutting policy issues (within and across organisations). These require 'integrating initiatives' and leadership to drive them. Their research suggests the need for strategies which are led from the centre of a local authority, politically underwritten and with partners involved from an early stage in order to develop a sense of common 'ownership'. Reid and Iqbal (*ESRC*) have been exploring the impact of such inter-organisational networks in the social housing field – albeit that those networks are more broadly based (involving statutory, private and voluntary organisations). They show the networks to be well developed and, although they make managerial life more difficult, are argued to make for a better quality of outcome.

This particular research suggests that, while their value is widely recognised, relationships within networks or partnerships are seldom studied. They see no reason to believe that there is anything peculiar about housing and point to two contrasting cultures in play. On the one hand, a competitive culture, which is flexible and entrepreneurial, involving only those who want to join. This is efficient (but not necessarily effective), shifting, changing and exclusive. In contrast there is a co-operative or collaborative culture, which deliberately sets out to be inclusive, consolidating resources, building relationships and emphasising co-ordination. This culture is more stable but less flexible – and probably produces more effective outcomes. The two patterns almost certainly demand different styles of behaviour and sets of skills.

The political debate about disaggregation has made much of the improvements which flow through to service delivery when there is focused dedication and enthusiasm. Pollit *et al.* (*ESRC*) are examining the impact of decentralised responsibility in hospitals, housing and education. They are able to show that greater autonomy produces benefit – at any rate in the perception of those to whom power is given. They note the problems for planning and co-ordination (their evidence only suggests it is more difficult) and for reduced accountability in conventional terms. However, their interim conclusions introduce two cautionary notes. First, while decentralisation has undoubtedly strengthened the institutions to which power is given, it has been matched by centralisation within those institutions. Whether this is a consequence of the early stages of newly acquired autonomy within a hospital or school or whether it is the start of a longer term pattern is not clear. Only research over time will tell us.

Secondly, the research underlines the problem of teasing out the impact on service effectiveness. Efficiency measures show an improvement, but this could be the result of the additional resources which have tended to accompany attempts to extend autonomy. The Audit Commission's review of LMS (*Audit Commission*: 1993a) confirms improvement in efficiency. Again, we may only be able to conclude that new patterns are evolving and that conclusions about the longer term are difficult. Equally, the research demonstrates the difficulty of evaluating the connection between new approaches to management and organisational form and policy outcomes. Interestingly, the various researchers feel unable to make a judgement about whether or not there has been 'deep-seated cultural change' – possibly another sign of the difficulty of short-range judgement in an evolving and rapidly adjusting situation.

In the educational field, collaborative relationships and their broader cultural setting have been examined in Wales by Farrell and Law (*Rowntree*: 1995) and in Scotland by Finlay (*Rowntree*: 1995). Farrell and Law, looking at the impact of education reforms on accountability in Wales conclude that Welsh political culture has prevented the shift to a 'strategic' LEA from going far. There has been resistance to market reforms (there are few GMS schools) with the consultative style of the education network placing high value on partnership and distinct Welsh identity. In Scotland, Finlay's work on relationships between LEAs and schools and colleges again suggests a less conflictual and competitive environment than England. This matches the generally perceived view of

Scotland as an environment less friendly to 'market' reforms and more in tune with traditional public service delivery.

Ranson *et al.* (*ESRC*) confirm the resistance of Scotland and Wales to the education reform process. They are concerned with changes in school management, but have a wider interest which focuses on the potential for the greater freedom of schools to foster involvement in civil society and to empower parents as full members of that society. They explore the institutional change necessary to reach agreement with parents and the community about the purposes and processes of learning – and confirm a passive political culture. They argue, therefore, that if the potential benefits of this aspect of decentralisation are to be gained, the rights and responsibilities of parents must be nurtured and fostered. Schools will need to mediate hard if consensus is to be reached and actively shared.

Empowerment

The Ranson *et al.* (*ESRC*) research takes us to a further theme: the empowerment of citizens and communities to act where, previously, government may have acted on their behalf. (This is central to the Osborne and Gaebler (1992) 're-invention' framework, though it is not part of the Hood typology (1990).) A range of projects impinge these ideas. Aldbourne Associates' (*Rowntree Housing*: 1995) evaluation of the transfer of Danish practices empowering tenants to an estate in Sutton LBC, while limited to a single case, confirms the importance of sound management, careful and extensive preparation, and considerable investment in training and IT. In short, the end cannot be achieved without willing the means. This confirms more general work on empowerment e.g. through decentralisation (Burns, Hambleton and Hoggett, 1994). The work by Clapham *et al.* (*ESRC*) on community ownership of housing carries a similar message. It also suggests higher levels of confidence and trust in these arrangements than in other democratic forms and reveals perceptions of improved service delivery among the tenants concerned. Once again, however, the researchers are nervous about drawing too general conclusions because the initiatives are limited – and young.

The involvement of (empowered) intermediary institutions are studied by Young (*ESRC*) and Barnes *et al.* (*ESRC*) among others. Young examines the role of not-for-private-profit organisations in environmental policy. He sees the potential to build a bottom-up approach to policy, with such organisations providing new avenues for involvement and participation and posing a new challenge to local authorities to find ways of engaging with them. If relationships with local government are good then real possibilities open up; if they are not, little will happen. In environmental policy at any rate, such relationships are fragile – but need to be seen as important in the differentiated world of local governance in which a whole range of actors and organisations are involved in environmental issues.

Barnes *et al.* (*ESRC*) also recognise the fragile nature of intermediary groups. In their case they are looking at user groups in the fields of mental health and disability and noting different patterns – in the former case an emphasis on advocacy and, in the latter, campaigning. Their interest in how such groups are received (and handled) by officials (awaiting further data and analysis at the time of writing) but they point to three possibilities – that such groups do not create a problem or that this is difficult too establish because 'politically correctness' defines their legitimacy, or that officials try to co-opt the groups into policy, management and service delivery processes so 'normalising' them. Again, at this stage of the research it is only possible to point to an evolving set of circumstances which requires further monitoring and evaluation.

Goss and Miller (*Rowntree*: 1995) examining the involvement of users in community care show the difficulty of making user empowerment work, but highlight the benefits which can accrue to service organisations and workers as well as users. Although a small-scale project, the conclusions suggest that more equal power relationships produce efficiency and also that user involvement ensures that services are better tailored to individual needs. The implication is that the lessons are widely applicable across local government.

Three pieces of work for the Commission for Local Democracy pursue a rather different tack and illustrate the importance of designing research to test expressed points of view. Geddes (*CLD*: 1995), exploring poverty and excluded communities, argues the importance of democratic local decision-making. Poor communities have been increasingly excluded from decision-making through the imposition of government-led regeneration initiatives with their appointed boards. While the argument is plausible it would be interesting to see it tested in local situations to see whether local democracy necessarily involves – and appointed bodies exclude – such communities. Phillips (*CLD*: 1994) displays similar normative arguments in a general review paper on local democracy, going on to press the case for new democratic mechanisms which recognise citizens and not just customers. For her, market choice is weaker than democratic choice.

The use of alternative democratic mechanisms to empower citizens is the focus for McNulty (*CLD*: 1995) in his work on referenda and citizens' ballots. Drawing on the Strathclyde water referendum, he argues the utility of such devices but suggests that they cannot be a 'bolt-on' device but have to be embedded in the political system. Using the American experience of citizens' ballots, McNulty goes on to trace the pressures for tightening fiscal regimes and the introduction of market-based mechanisms and private sector management techniques. In this way some of the influences pushing towards a 'new public management' are thus being reinforced by the citizen empowerment which is one of its functions! Paradoxically, of course, the strengthening of local democracy and citizen empowerment would also be supported by those working to constrain a new managerialism, thus complicating the argument still further – but that takes us outside the remit of this paper. There is also no reason to believe that the American experience would necessarily be repeated in the UK.

Performance and quality
Definitions of the 'new' management consistently place emphasis on performance and on outputs and outcomes (compared to the traditional concern with inputs). The 1992 organisational change survey (*LGMB*: Young, 1993) reveals the extent to which performance issues were establishing themselves on the local authority agenda with 92 per cent of councils having established performance reporting mechanisms. The 1994 survey (*LGMB*: 1996) shows the momentum maintained (with the figure of 96 per cent). Interestingly enough, however, there is no evidence that a results orientation was having an impact on individual pay. In 1992, 80 per cent of the white-collar workforce were not covered by PRP schemes: in 1994 the figures was 81 per cent. For chief executives, chief officers and senior grades the proportions had actually declined.

The Audit Commission and the LGMB have been leading protagonists for performance management. They have both undertaken field research to monitor the extent of its use. The work of both organisations is thus set in a prescriptive context, even though performance management is a term used to capture a number of different elements, for example LGMB's *People and Performance* (*LGMB*: 1993) defines it as a systematic approach linking strategy and service objectives to jobs and people, involving clear collective and individual work objectives, performance indicators and measurement, appraisal, and, often, performance-related pay; the Audit Commission set a broader agenda in *Calling the Tune* (1995) which involves specification – including objectives, milestones, targets, communication (outside to the public and internal to the organisation) and evaluation – which tracks the performance of individuals, teams and whole organisations. The fieldwork which both organisations have undertaken suggests that very few councils have rejected the idea of performance management – 7 per cent according to the LGMB (1993) with another 1 per cent (three councils) withdrawing after having a go.

While the Audit Commission have gone on to track the potential of performance management approaches to reduce the paybill, improve productivity and seek improvement in organisational and job design arrangements (e.g. *Audit Commission*: 1995b and 1995c) there is little systematic evidence available of the impact on service delivery and policy effectiveness. The same is true for the extensive work done on performance indicators. Rhetoric and anecdote are quick to ally measurement with improvement (and this, of course, lies at the heart of the Citizens' Charter movement). A range of published work draws on the Commission's research and development activity in this area (e.g. *Audit Commission*: 1992, 1993b, 1994, 1995d) but most of this is concerned with the design of indicators and results of their use. Major questions remain about what and how to measure and about how measurement information is used.

The Pollitt *et al.* (*ESRC*) research is one of the few pieces of work which explicitly sets out to assess the impact of new approaches to management on policy outcomes. As we have already noted the results are equivocal. Efficiency measures show improvement but the causation is not clear – is it new patterns of management or additional resources – or something else – which makes the difference? The research team argues that effectiveness will take longer to measure. The evaluation of 'bottom-up' approaches (Aldbourne (Rowntree: 1995); Clapham *et al.*, (*ESRC*)) suggest improved quality of service as a result of the changes but more systematic work is clearly needed.

As striking as anything in the last few years has been the interest in quality and developing management approaches to enhancing quality. The LGMB 1992 (*LGMB*: Young, 1993) and 1994 (*LGMB*: 1996) surveys demonstrate the growth in this interest. In 1994, 55 per cent of authorities reported authority-wide 'charter' statements or the like (compared with 29 per cent in 1992); and policies on quality in particular services in 75 per cent of councils (compared with 49 per cent in 1992). There is no doubting the growth of interest which has been echoed in the much published expectations of central government, the Audit Commission, the LGMB and the local authority associations. A large literature has also emerged; Gaster (1994) is a good example of work which pulls together the issues as they impact on public service and indicates the sources of research and intelligence on the various dimensions of quality. There remains difficulty, yet again, in getting behind the rhetoric to discern the impact in service effectiveness.

Managing change

Running through most of the research which touches on a new or developing public management is, inevitably, a theme of change and its management. Lowndes *et al. (ESRC)* have, explicitly, explored the nature of change in local public management and the reasons for it. The project has looked at change within organisations and the management across networks of organisations – and the implications of that for citizens and democracy. Although it has not yet reported, the project usefully draws attention to the multi-level nature of change processes and to the internal tensions and conflicts which exist as change is explored and takes place.

Old and new institutional forms vie with one or another and often pull in opposite directions, sometimes at the same time: for example, contracts and user-involvement clash with traditional departmental arrangements and professionalism; centralisation and decentralisation can both be part of the same organisation development strategy; political processes and market choice both claim to be legitimate channels of public accountability; and so on. One of the central questions the researchers seem to be posing is whether we are at the point of fundamental change in public management or at just another stage of adaptation or evolution – as was suggested in the opening section of this paper. The researchers have, incidentally, tracked the coverage of changing ideas about management in the local government and NHS trade and professional press over a 12-year period and found a shifting focus of interest and in the language used – and one which accords with themes recognisably part of the orthodoxy of the 'new public management'.

There are also clues in the research which appear to confirm the forces behind management change in local government and which shed light on the processes of change. In the report of their 1992 survey of organisational change, Young and Mills (*LGMB*: 1993) paint a picture of government legislation and centrally inspired financial restraint more or less overwhelming local government and driving the search for new approaches. So uniform was the conclusion of that survey that the second survey in 1994 did not even attempt to re-visit the issue. It would be interesting to know whether the earlier wave of change has produced its own momentum (and an appetite) for voluntarily inspired change in the last couple of years. As they stand, the conclusions do not seem to match the *Re-inventing Government* story of innovative managers eagerly searching out a new kind of management! Equally, the survey did not match the anecdotal evidence of a new generation of managers relishing the excuse of an external threat to create internal changes, whether driven by a coherent philosophy or not.

However, that anecdotal evidence seems to be borne out by the conclusions of another piece of LGMB-commissioned research (from INLOGOV, *LGMB:* 1993) which explored the characteristics of good management in 16 local authorities selected as 'well managed' by peer assessment. This underlined the importance of good managers and organisational leaders in shaping the change process and conveys the impression of such people actively using the external pressures to re-shape their organisation to meet locally defined purpose. Interestingly too, that research used case-study managers' own words to contrast a 'new' management with an 'old' one. The language of the new – defined in 1992 before Osborne and Gaebler reached the UK and, indeed, before the idea of a 'new public management' had become commonplace – matches both. The new language and new ways were seen as emerging from the old to meet the new environment of the 1990's; there was no suggestion, though, that it professed an intellectual coherence, however 'good' it was thought to be.

The process of change is also captured in the research on the 16 authorities. Shared values and culture, strategy, staff development, and the secondary place of structure and systems emerge as key features of getting the change process right. These are themes which recurred in the major LGMB project *Fitness for Purpose* (LGMB:1993) which used the experience of organisational change to argue the need for organisations (structures, processes, systems and people) to be designed and marshalled to serve strategic direction or purpose.

The business of managing change has been the subject of further study sponsored by the LGMB and carried out at Warwick University (*LGMB:* Hartley *et al.*, 1995). Looking at the experience of six councils and at a range of different kinds of changes, the project emphasises the importance of leadership (managerial and political), of culture (but distinguishing between focusing on culture as a mechanism for change and responding to cultural change issues as a by-product of a structural and operational agenda), of vision and strategy and of a range of more practical issues such as timing, handling conflict and opposition and 'change support processes'. This underscores the complexity of handling organisational change. It is also confirmed by work MORI did for LGMB in 1993 (*LGMB:* 1994) on attitudes to the handling of change in which managers are criticised for their poor performance – not least for apparently failing to think through and hold together the various facets of change and for failing to communicate and secure an understanding of what is going on.

Professionalisation of management
The 'professionalisation' of management and the separation of professional management from political management are defined as characteristics of the

'new' public management. The 1980s and 1990s have seen great emphasis placed on the importance of high quality management in local government. Successive reports and statements from the Audit Commission, the LGMB, the local authority associations and the like have underscored this need. The Audit Commission have recently been considering the extent to which this is supported by a rigorous approach to training and development; work in this area will build on the evidence collected for their work on performance management (*Audit Commission*: 1995a, 1995b and 1995c). The 1992 Organisational Change Survey (*LGMB*: Young, 1993) shows the extent to which increased resource commitments for management development had been made in the preceding three years, a finding which will probably be confirmed by the more recent survey.

The early 1990s have also seen more systematic attention given to management training and development in general. The work of the national Management Charter Initiative and the setting of levels of management competence (for management across all sectors) is a hallmark of a general movement towards professionalism. The LGMB and large numbers of individual local authorities hold unpublished information about the spread of this movement but, as yet, there is no systematic survey, either of the extent of its spread or of its impact. An important part of this movement has been emphasis on defining management competences. The thrust of much of this work aligns the competences with a great deal of the new management, much of it being developed in the private sector.

Crucial to the local government is the relationship between the paid professional managers and political management. A major survey of 1600 councillors was conducted by Young and Rao in 1993 (*Rowntree*: 1993). This confirmed the amount of time spent on their work by councillors (not far short of 20 hours a week), half of which is spent in council, committee and other formal meetings or related preparatory discussions with much of the business being managerial. The Audit Commission (*Audit Commission*: 1990) had undertaken work which had revealed a similar pattern, pleading for serious consideration to be given to matching political processes and structures to the roles played by councillors. The LGMB has published a series of papers, notably arising from work undertaken by John Stewart, which has drawn the same conclusion.

The Young and Rao study (*Rowntree*: 1993) shows remarkable similarity in the time spent by councillors on 'management' issues across all kinds of local authority and between 'frontbenchers' and 'backbenchers'. A number of observers, however, have commented on the way in which councillors feel marginalised by the professionalisation of management and by the changes of the new public management – confirmed by the work from the DoE (*DoE*: Walker, 1993) and Rowntree (*Rowntree*: Rao and Young, 1995) on competitive tendering, both of which touch on the role of elected members. Surprisingly, however, the Young and Rao study suggests a high level of satisfaction with current decision-making arrangements. The clue here may be the suspicion of changes which might further concentrate power in the hands of a minority of (frontbench) councillors or increase delegation to officers. This repeated the findings of an earlier study by Rao (*Rowntree*: 1992).

Rowntree also funded research from Young (*Rowntree*: 1994) on what might be learned from international comparison. This work concentrated on strong executive systems (mayoral systems in Germany, France and the USA and city-manager arrangements in the USA) but concluded that the intensity of resistance to change in Britain made such systems unlikely to find support here. Projects designed to explore increased patterns of turnover (*Rowntree*: Bloch, 1992 and Kerley, 1992) also confirmed that little attention was being given to meeting the frustrations of many retiring councillors about the way their role was being conducted and supported.

Notwithstanding this apparent reluctance to contemplate radical change – and the apparent support for the status quo – the LGMB organisational change surveys suggest that some change is happening. Committees are reducing in number and frequency of meeting and there is greater use of working parties and panels – many of which have shared officer/councillor membership. This information on political processes might be taken as a signal of councillors 'professionalising' *their* contribution to strategic issues and policy development and to a clarification of roles and relationships between officers and councillors. Clearly, more detailed exploration of this is needed before such conclusion is possible, given the weight of evidence pointing in the opposite direction.

'Steering not rowing'
Despite its various definitions the new public management is deemed to place emphasis on the strategic or enabling role of the local authority. The Alexander work on fragmentation (*LGMB*:1993) and the more recent research by Leach, Clarke *et al.* (*LGMB*: 1996) demonstrate the tension between traditional service provision and more strategic enabling roles, but in the case of the latter it shows the extent to which the idea of community governance and the strategic local authority has become a predominant model. This seems to be confirmed – at least in some areas – by the findings of the LGMB organisational change

surveys. Looking at the role of the LEA the survey showed a marked shift between 1988 and 1994 – the traditional provision role as the principal one reducing from 76 per cent to 31 per cent, with that of 'partner' rising from 54 per cent to 82 per cent and 'enabler' from 46 per cent to 72 per cent. The LGMB report from John Stewart (*LGMB*: 1995) confirms this shift in the way in which local authorities see themselves, though he also points to the multiplexity of roles. The Lowndes *et al.* (*ESRC*) project will explore some of the implications for the way in which local authorities (among others) manage themselves in this environment.

A less optimistic picture is painted by Jervis and Richards (1995). Looking more widely than local government, they conclude that the British experience shows that while significant efficiency ('rowing') improvements have resulted from new management change, strategic opportunities to improve effectiveness have been missed. Their contention is that government and politicians find it difficult to stop 'rowing' and to resist intervening. Distancing provision and keeping it at arm's length from politicians, re-defined as 'enablers', 'purchasers' or 'commissioners', may provide increased managerial 'space' but 'since the provision of public service remains contested, politicians have been unable to withdraw from the arena'. Jervis and Richards go on to postulate an argument that a new kind of model of strategic management, 'value driven ... (and allowing) the articulation and resolution of conflicting aspirations and imperatives' is needed. They would argue that the translation of operational management approaches from private to public management is easier than strategic ones. Given the interest and emphasis on the role of the local authority in the arena of local governance, this kind of fundamental question should be a priority for further exploration.

Consistency, coherence and issues arising

To comment on the consistency and coherence of the research findings is not straightforward. Self-evidently the research does not have – and could not be expected to have – either the consistency or coherence which might be expected from a targeted or carefully designed programme. Issues of management are often incidental and the 'new public management' is seldom expressly addressed, let alone is there analysis and evaluation of its impact. Even those pieces of research which set out to provide some kind of mapping of the situation (e.g. *LGMB*: Young, 1993, 1996) have neither been comprehensive nor, for that matter, specifically concerned with the new public management. Moreover, there are a series of elements usually associated with the 'new' public management not touched on in the research (which are returned to below in the discussion of future work).

The position is further complicated by the fact that much of the research of recent years is only just emerging, or is often not yet reported in final published form, or even still in progress. Equally, many of the management innovations and changes which can be taken to characterise the 'new' public management are still young and being fashioned. One of the most consistent features of the research, therefore, is that more questions are asked than answered. Even in areas where there has been a lot of work (e.g. competition and contracting), while there may be consistency in description of what has happened, major questions are left about such things as impact, the nature of contractual relationships, the capacity of emerging arrangements to survive changed circumstances, etc. In others areas, where closer attention has been given to the impact of management change (e.g. *ESRC: Pollitt et al.*), it is difficult to know whether short-term impact will last into the longer term or whether the consequences of change will shift over time.

This points to two further issues which are common to much of the research. First, most of it is inevitably time limited and therefore only captures one 'snapshot'. Given what was said earlier about the evolving nature of management ideas and practice, this is a major limitation. All of the themes require study over time to capture both their evolution and the changing impact of approaches or practices. To take Pollitt *et al.* (*ESRC*) again, NHS trusts, LMS and devolution of management responsibility to hospitals or schools may decentralise within the health authority or LEA but centralise within the hospital or school – but it also may be that this will modify over time and with an increase in security and confidence. Early and certain conclusions may be dangerous; change needs to be monitored over time.

Secondly, the fact that management is only the means to an end must never be lost sight of. Public management – and organisations for that matter – are no more than the means to delivering public policy objectives. They may be important – and may have an independent impact on effectiveness and outcomes – but they are only part of the story. That is not a reason to stop taking them seriously, but it is a reminder that the content and substance of what is intended should always be a primary consideration. The most effective organisation and best management cannot substitute for poor policy. To be consumed by questions about whether elements of a 'new' public management are good or bad is less important than seeking to determine whether they help or hinder particular programmes or projects. The fact that management is largely incidental to much of the research under scrutiny is essentially not a criticism and may even be a strength. The repeated implication that more systematic and evaluative research is needed should be tempered by the need to maintain a broader perspective.

If there cannot be expected to be an overall consistency and coherence in the research, we have at least noted some internal consistency within each of the themes. Where there are multiple pieces of work with a similar focus there is more similarity than difference in findings – though we also noted a number of apparently significant discrepancies. That in itself is an argument for further work. This issue is pursued further on pages 63–5.

Future implications

Implications for local government powers, rules and structures; and for central–local relations

Although the aspects of the research which touch on the new public management have no direct implication for the formal constitutional position of local government and the central–local relationship, there are a number of issues which indirectly arise:

- The emphasis on organisational disaggregation and on competition, with its consequences for mixed economies of public service provision, underline the plural nature of local governance. The research implicitly raises questions about how this is best managed, about the relationships which underpin it and, inevitably, about the role of the local authority. These questions feed a broader debate about what is implied by the idea of local governance, its consequences for the local authority and the structures and processes needed to support it. None of the research does more than fuel the debate – but the debate is important.

- The question of the structure of local government is currently dominated by the reorganisation of local government in Scotland and Wales and by the partial reorganisation in England. Two sets of questions arise from the research. The first is about what can be learned from it to assist the creation of new organisations and managerial patterns. Though only partial, there are a whole series of points, drawn from each of the themes discussed, which have practical implications for the design of new arrangements. These range from the impact of competition and its management, through the need for integration and so on, to member arrangements. The second set of questions is to do with the continuation of two-tier local government in England and whether there are pointers in the research which would assist its improvement. The answers here are less obvious, but again there are clues about styles of relationships, new skills and processes to develop collaborative working and partnership, and the like, which are worth taking seriously.

- A third set of issues relate to the way in which any local authority discharges its functions and responsibilities. Even taking into account the fact that much of the research is incomplete and much of it time-limited, the conclusions and results reported above point to a body of information and experience about management and organisational issues and the way in which they are most helpfully addressed. Again, each of the themes throws up questions which need to be asked as new and different patterns of management are explored.

- So far as the central–local relationship is concerned, the material takes us back to a core document of the Joseph Rowntree Foundation Local and Central Government Relations Research Committee, *A New Accord* (*Rowntree*: 1992), and its plea for better learning across the central–local divide. There are two key points here. Firstly, since much of the new management is to do with approaches and activities common to central as well as local government, there needs to be free exchange of experience and learning. All the evidence suggests that little of this happens. This needs to change. Issues to do with competition and markets, disaggregation and integration, performance and quality, the professionalisation of management and strategic management seem especially pertinent. Secondly, the need for better understanding and the fact of a shared agenda suggest the need for more co-operation between the two sides as changes are promoted or encouraged. Much of the research touches on what is, in effect, part of local government's response to the changes forced by legislation. Such changes should, ideally, be the consequence of joint exploration and agreement between local and central government. Of course there will always be political pressures which force part of the agenda and unbalance the relationship, but these should not inhibit the search for collaboration and partnership.

Implications for current and future policy

The point was made at the end of the section on the research itself that, while the focus of this paper is on management issues, such considerations should be secondary. Management and organisation are only the means to an end. However, both can obviously have an impact on the effectiveness with which policy objectives are pursued. Good management or organisation are no substitute for poor policy, but good policy can be undermined by poor management. Three particular points arise:

- In any area of policy it is important to know how best to implement and deliver objectives – whether this involves 'newer' or 'older' management approaches. Part of the framing and development of policy should therefore be careful judgement about appropriate management arrangements. Too often these may be ill thought through or rest on simple assertions which set the direction without sufficient evidence or experience to support them – e.g. the use of market-testing or competitive mechanisms, decentralisation, etc. in appropriate settings.

• Following from this there must be an implication about experimentation as compared to comprehensive or wholescale reform. Given the uncertainty surrounding many of the 'new' management developments and questions about the longer-term impact of some of the ideas, there are strong arguments for policy change using experiments which are evaluated carefully before general moves are made. This is important against the background of a decade and more during which wholesale reform has been fashionable.

• The third issue is different and relates to questions about how best to encourage or initiate change. The Osborne and Gaebler (1992) model is of self-motivated 'entrepreneurial' managers largely pushing forward the boundaries. The British position, on the other hand, is one where local government has changed a great deal – but in response to an external threat. Whether or not there is an independent momentum is difficult to judge. It should be in the interests of both local and central government to encourage a situation where change is self-motivated and happens because it is desired or the need for it is recognised. The question is how this is best achieved.

Implications for research

The review has inevitably been limited and selective. It has taken examples of current and recent research, sponsored by the major funders, which relate to the 'new public management' – and it has done that against an interpretation of the latter as being part of the continuing evolution of management ideas and approaches. In doing this the review has noted that the relevant (general) management literature is full of assertion – which has been ably embraced by the rhetoric of politicians and managers alike. In these circumstances one of the major implications must be for more systematic research. There is a need to track and evaluate the impact of different elements of the new (or, indeed, any) public management and to tease out what approaches are best related to what circumstances. Indeed, one attractive possibility would be the establishment of a focused programme of research dedicated to doing this. If such a programme were not sufficiently important to any one research funder, a carefully orchestrated collaborative programme *between* funders might be designed.

Through the discussion of the various themes, indication of areas for further research will have been clear. Examples of these themes will be highlighted to demonstrate the kind of research agenda which is outstanding. First, however, two general points:

- The importance of mapping management and organisational change will have been evident. The LGMB survey needs to be maintained and efforts made to ensure that it is as comprehensive as possible. Other funders and individual researchers should be encouraged to shape its coverage.

- Systematic work is also needed to explore the extent of coherence or contradiction between management approaches.

As far as the individual themes go, examples include:

- *competition* – the need to examine different models of contractual relationships (particularly less formal ones) between purchasers and providers; exploration of how far market models can be taken in relation to public service provision without changing the latter beyond recognition

- *disaggregation* – examination of the relative strengths and weaknesses of single- and multi-purpose organisations; the means available for integration where there are multiple organisations working alongside one another, and evaluation of emerging practice; the skills and processes involved in successful partnerships and collaborative working

- *empowerment* – the effectiveness and impact of mechanisms which build from the bottom-up, empowering service users or citizens, and the circumstances in which different approaches are appropriate; the consequences of 'empowerment' for attitudes towards, and identity with, government institutions and processes; relationships between new approaches to empowerment and traditional democratic practices

- *performance and quality* – evaluation of different approaches to performance management and the impact of delivery; the use of performance measurement and its impact; the use of different approaches to quality and the impact of e.g. citizens' charter practices on service effectiveness

- *change management* – mention has already been made of exploring the drivers of change; there is an equally important question about the inhibitors to change. Though in no sense exclusive to the ideas of the 'new' public management questions about what stops new approaches being explored is as interesting as what prompts them

- *professionalisation of management* – the work on management competences is new and so its impact is uncharted; assessment and evaluation is needed. The effects of managerialism and professional management, as opposed to the traditional management by professionals, needs careful exploration; as does the way in which member–officer relations are developing and whether new styles of working (suggested in the LGMB survey) are changing the previously well documented conventions

- *strategic management* – an assessment of 'steering' as opposed to 'rowing' capacities and the relationship between the two, and an evaluation of the impact of such approaches where they have been adopted, not least to test the emerging ideas of Jervis and Richards (1995) quoted in the text.

There are, then, a series of themes associated with the definition of the 'new' public management which have received little attention in the research. In particular:

- the extent of use of private sector management styles and their compatibility with the tasks of the public sector at the local level

- the impact of a 'parsimonious' approach to resources, the way in which this is handled, decisions made and results evaluated

- the use of greater flexibility in pay and conditions of service and their effects

- the regulatory role of local government – particularly in relation to the development of markets and mixed economies of service provision.

In short, there is a substantial agenda of potential research with local public management as its focus. Two challenges arise. The first will be to ensure that it is approached in as systematic and rigorous a way as possible. The second, as it addresses and evaluates the orthodoxy which has emerged, will be to point to ways in which public management might evolve. 'For each age is a dream that is dying/or one that is coming to birth' (Arthur O'Shaughnessey). Paradigm shift may be exaggerated but constant change and adaptation is undeniably right. Practice and research both show – and will continue to show – strengths and weaknesses, dilemmas and inconsistencies. Part of the feedback from research to practice is confirmation and/or demonstration; part should be to offer pointers (not prescription) to the future.

Bibliography

Aucoin, P. (1993) 'Administrative reform in public management: paradigms, principles, paradoxes and pendulums', *Governance*

Ayres, I. and Braithwaite, J. (1992) *Responsive Regulation.* Oxford: Oxford University Press

Barzealey, M. (1992) *Breaking Through Bureaucracy: A New Vision for Managing in Government.* Berkeley: University of California Press

Bozeman, B. (ed.) (1994) *Public Management.* San Francisco: Jossey-Bass

Burns, D., Hambleton, R. and Hoggett, P. (1994) *The Politics of Decentralisation.* London: Macmillan

Carnaghan, R. and Bracewell-Milnes, B. (1993) *Testing the Market.* Institute for Economic Affairs

Clarke, M. (1994) *The New Management Agenda.* Scotland: SOLACE

Clarke, M. (1996) *Renewing Public Management.* London: Pitmans

Commission for Local Democracy (1995) *Taking Charge: The Rebirth of Local Democracy*

Dilulio, J., Garvey, G. and Kern, D. (1994) *Improving Government Performance.* Washington: Brookings

Dunleavy, P. and Hood, C. (1994) 'From old public administration to new public management', *Public Money and Management*, vol. 14, no. 3, July–September

Dunleavy, P. and Massey, A. (1995) 'British public management: achievements, problems and prospects', *Public Policy and Administration*, vol. 10 no. 2, Summer

Dunsire, A. (1995) 'Administrative theory in the 1980s: a view point', *Public Administration*, vol. 73, no.1, Spring,

Flynn, N. 'Public sector management in Europe: some trends and tendencies' (From *Public Sector Management in Europe*, forthcoming)

Foster, C. (1992) *Privatisation, Public Ownership and the Regulation of National Monopoly*. Oxford: Blackwell

Francis, J. (1993) *The Politics of Regulation*. Oxford: Blackwell

Gaster, L. (1994) *Quality In Public Services*. Buckingham: Open University Press

Goodsell, C. (1994) *The Case for Bureaucracy*. London: Chatham House

le Grand, J. and Bartlett, W. (1993) *Quasi-markets and Social Policy*. London: Macmillan

Gray, A. and Jenkins, B. (1995) 'From public administration to public management: reassessing a revolution?', *Public Administration*, vol. 73, no. 1, Spring

Harden, I. (1992) *The Contracting State*. Buckingham: Open University Press

Hood, C. (1990) *Beyond the Public Bureaucracy State? Public Administration in the 1990s*, Inaugural Lecture, London School of Economics

Hood, C. (1991) 'A public management for all seasons?', *Public Administration*. vol. 69, no.1, Spring

Hood, C. (1995) 'Emerging issues in public administration', *Public Administration*. vol. 73, no. 1, Spring

Hood, C. (1995) 'Contemporary public management: a new global paradigm?', *Public Policy and Administration*, vol. 10, no. 2, Summer

Hood, C. and Jackson, M. (1991) *Administrative Argument*. Dartmouth

Ingraham, P. and Romzek, B. (1994) *New Paradigms for Government*. San Francisco: Jossey-Bass

Jervis, P. and Richards, S. (1995) 'Strategic management in re-invented government: rowing 1, steering 0', Paper presented to Strategic Management Society Conference, Mexico City

Judge, D., Stoker, G. and Wolman, H. (1995) *Theories of Urban Politics*. Sage

Kay, J. (1994) *Foundations of Corporate Success*. Oxford: OUP

Kerley, R. (1995) *Managing Local Government*. London: Macmillan

Kettl, D. and Dilulio, J. (eds) (1995) *Inside the Reinvention Machine*. Washington: Brookings

Kettl, D. (1993) *Sharing Power*. Washington: Brookings

Kuhn, T. (1970) *The Structure of Scientific Revolutions*. Chicago: Chicago UP

Leach, S., Walsh, K. *et al.* (1993) *Challenge and Change: Characteristics of Good Management in Local Government*. LGMB

Osborne, D. and Gaebler, T. (1992) *Reinventing Government*. Reading, Mass: Addison-Wesley

Peters, G. and Savoie, D. (eds) (1995) *Governance in a Changing Environment*. Ottawa: Canadian Centre for Management Development

Peters, T. and Waterman, R. (1984) *In Search of Excellence*. New York: Harper and Row

Pollitt, C. (1993) (second edition) *Managerialism and the Public Service*. Oxford: Blackwell

Salamon, L. (1995) *Partners in Public Service*. Baltimore: Johns Hopkins University Press

Savoie, D. (1994) *Thatcher, Reagan, Mulroney: In Search of a New Bureaucracy*. Pitsburg: Pitsburg University Press

Stewart, J. *et al.* (1995) *The Changing Organisation and Management of Local Government*. London: Macmillan

Walsh, K. (1995) *Public Service and Market Mechanisms*. London: Macmillan

Walsh, K. and Stewart, J. (1992) 'The new management of public services', *Public Administration*

Research projects

The Economic and Social Research Council

The following projects form part of the Local Governance Programme, now drawing to a close. This review draws on the unpublished papers, for the most part; in particular on papers prepared for a Programme conference which took place at the University of Exeter in September 1995.

The Performance of Autonomous Local Service Delivery Agencies
Christopher Pollitt, Johnston Birchall, Keith Putman (Centre for the Evaluation of Public Policy and Defence, Brunel University)

New Forms of Education Management
Stuart Ranson, Jane Martin (The University of Birmingham)
Jon Nixon (University of Sheffield)
Penny McKewan (University of Ulster)

Consumerism and Citizenship Amongst Users of Health and Social Care Services
Steve Harrison, Gerald Wistow (Nuffield Institute for Health, University of Leeds)
Marian Barnes (Department of Sociological Studies, University of Sheffield)

Economic Culture and Local Governance
Maureen Mackintosh, Madeleine Wahlberg (Faculty of Social Science, The Open University)

The New Management, Citizenship and Institutional Change in Local Governance
Vivien Lowndes, Jackie Woollam (INLOGOV, University of Birmingham)
Kathryn Riley (Roehampton Institute)

Inter-organisational Relationships and the Delivery of Housing Services
Barbara Reid, Barbara Iqbal (Department of Environmental Health and Housing, University of Salford)

Local Strategies for Crime Prevention: Co-ordination and Accountability
John Benyon, Alan Edwards (Centre for Study of Public Order, University of Leicester)

The Commission For Local Democracy

Local Democracy: the Terms of the Debate
Anne Phillips, 1994

The Role and Purpose of Local Government
Gerry Stoker (University of Strathclyde), 1994

Poverty, Excluded Communities and Local Democracy
Mike Geddes (University of Warwick), 1995

Referenda and Citizens' Ballots
Des McNulty (Glasgow Caledonian University), 1995

The Local Government Management Board

Who Uses Local Services? Striving For Equity
Glenn Bramley and Julian Le Grand (Belgrave Paper 4), 1992

Managing Fragmentation
Alan Alexander (University of Strathclyde), 1993

A Portrait of Change: 1992 Organisational Change Survey
Ken Young (Queen Mary and Westfield College, University of London), 1993. Report of 1994 survey (presented to 1995 PAC Conference) forthcoming at time of writing; central findings presented in a paper but subsequently published, 1996

Is the Citizens' Charter a Charter for Citizens?
David Prior, John Stewart, Kieron Walsh (Belgrave Paper 7), 1993

People and Performance
LGMB Guide, 1993

Fitness for Purpose
Michael Clarke *et al.*, 1993

Employee Attitudes to Local Government
Local Government Management Board/MORI, 1994

Influence and Influencing
Michael Clarke and John Stewart (INLOGOV, The University of Birmingham), 1994

Public–Private Partnerships
M. Parkinson, V. Roberts, and H. Russell (Liverpool John Moores University), 1995

Decentralisation and Devolution
J. Chandler, M. Gregory, M. Hunt and R. Turner (Sheffield Business School), 1995

Organisational and Cultural Change: A Qualitative Review
John Benington *et al.* (Warwick Business School), 1995

How Others See Us
Michael Clarke (Belgrave Paper 13), 1995

Combating Local Poverty
Peter Alcock *et al.* (Sheffield Hallam University), 1995

Local Government Today – An Observers View
John Stewart (INLOGOV, The University of Birmingham), 1995

Markets, Service and Choice
Kieron Walsh and John Stewart (Belgrave Paper 12), 1995

Managing Institutional and Cultural Change
Jean Hartley, Phillipa Cordingley and John Benington (Local Government Centre, University of Warwick), 1995

Minimising Fragmentation – Managing Services: Leading Communities
Steve Leach, Michael Clarke *et al.*, (INLOGOV The University of Birmingham), 1996

Changing Local Governance: Local Authorities and Non-Elected Agencies
Chris Painter *et al.* (University of Central England), 1996

The Department of the Environment

Competition for Building Maintenance: Direct Labour Organisations and Compulsory Competitive Tendering
Bruce Walker (INLOGOV University of Birmingham), HMSO 1993

Competition and Service: The Impact of the Local Government Act 1988
Kieron Walsh and Howard Davis (University of Birmingham), HMSO 1993

CCT: The Private Sector View
BMRB International Limited, DoE 1995

Analysis of Local Authority CCT Markets
Ernst and Young, DoE 1995.

The Joseph Rowntree Foundation

(a)   Local and Central Government Relations Research Committee

A New Accord
Sir Charles Carter with Peter John, 1992

Managing Change: Councillors and the New Local Government
Nirmala Rao (Queen Mary and Westfield College, University of London), 1992

The Turnover of Local Councils
Alice Bloch, 1992

Councillor Turnover in Scotland
Richard Kerley (University of Strathclyde), 1992

Coming to Terms with Change? The Local Government Councillor in 1993
Ken Young and Nirmala Rao (Queen Mary and Westfield College, University of London), 1994

A Positive Role for Local Government – Lessons from Other Countries
Joseph Rowntree Foundation Seminar, 1994

Local Leadership and Decision-making: A Study of France, Germany, the United States and Britain
Ken Young (Queen Mary and Westfield College, University of London), 1994

Educational Accountability in Wales
Catherine Farrell and Jenifer Law, 1995

Current Relationships between Local Authorities, Colleagues and Schools in Scotland
Ian Finlay (University of Strathclyde), 1995

Local Government: Lessons from Other Countries
Coopers and Lybrand, 1995

The Scope for Choice and Variety in Local Government
Mike Geddes (Local Government Centre, Warwick University), 1995

Local Authority Experience and Compulsory Competitive Tendering
Nirmala Rao and Ken Young (Queen Mary and Westfield College, University of London), 1995

(b)   Other Joseph Rowntree Research

The Feasibility of 'Residents' Democracy'
Aldbourne Associates, 1995

From Margin to Mainstream
Sue Goss and Clive Miller (Office for Public Management), 1995

The Audit Commission
The Audit Commission is legally charged with value-for-money auditing (economy, efficiency and effectiveness) and for promoting improved management performance. It publishes a wide range of material drawing on the work of its auditors and specially commissioned studies into particular aspects of local government management. Some of this work has been drawn on in this paper – both by way of example and where it confirms, amplifies or cuts across parallel academic research.

We Can't Go On Meeting Like This
HMSO, 1990

Citizens' Charter Indicators
HMSO, 1992

Adding Up the Sums
HMSO, 1993(a)

Staying on Course: The Second Year of Citizens Charter Indicators
HMSO, 1993(b)

Watching their Figures
HMSO, 1994

Calling the Tune
HMSO, 1995(a)

Paying the Piper
HMSO, 1995(b)

People, Pay and Performance
HMSO, 1995(c)

Local Authority Performance Indicators
HMSO, 1995(d) (3 volumes)

3 The impact of local government changes on the voluntary and community sectors

Marilyn Taylor

Introduction

The voluntary sector sees this time of change for local government as an opportunity to examine its own role and to define its place in local democracy
(Local Government Management Board,
Introducing the Voluntary Sector, 1995)

Background

The considerable changes in the structure and role of local government over recent years in the UK have been widely documented. A new language – of enabling, contracting and partnership – has become commonplace and responsibility for the development, resourcing and implementation of policy is shared among a range of local actors.

As the boundaries shift between public and private responsibility for welfare, voluntary and community organisations find themselves in the spotlight. Government policies require them to take a more prominent role in service delivery, offering an 'alternative' to the state. But of equal importance, as concepts of citizenship, civil society and local democracy are examined and redefined, is their role in contributing to public debate and in engaging a range of people in public life.

In Britain the increasing prominence given to the voluntary and community organisations is accompanied by the erosion of local government powers, with the sector posed as an alternative to the state. In other parts of continental Europe, this has not been the case. In part, this reflects the 'extent to which British local government is regarded almost exclusively as an institution for the delivery of services' (Blair, 1993), in comparison with much of Europe. It has much more to lose. But it also reflects the different approach to welfare reform and to national–local government relations taken in other European countries. In France and Italy, for example, the growth of the voluntary sector has been associated with the decentralisation of powers from central to local government.

This paper will review what is known about the impact of the changes in UK local government on the voluntary and community sectors by looking at recent and current research in the UK. It will introduce the review by summarising the current reforms and looking briefly at the changing relationship between the state and the voluntary sector[1] in the past. It will then examine the impact of current changes under two main headings. First, it will ask how the changes have affected the role of voluntary and community organisations as 'partners in service' and the contribution they make to the delivery of welfare in any locality. Secondly, it will look at the impact on their political role, as partners in policy-making: as a vehicle for public participation in policy development, as a vehicle for representing a diversity of interests and as contributors to public knowledge and debate. It will close by identifying the key themes arising from the review and their implications for further research.

Local government reform

The changes in local government have been extensively documented (Batley and Stoker, 1993; Stewart and Stoker, 1995). Those most relevant to this review are:

- measures to bypass local authorities through the creation of non-elected QUANGOs at local level and opportunities for devolved direct control of services through 'opting out'

- restrictions on local government powers to raise their own finance and new forms of inspection and review

- the creation of quasi-markets in welfare which separate purchasing and provider roles and encourage (or in the case of compulsory competitive tendering, require) the purchase of public services from independent (voluntary and private sector) providers

- the requirement that local government operate in partnership with other organisations, e.g. in bidding for Single Regeneration Budget (SRB) funds

- the 'new management': an emphasis on performance measures, audit and 'value for money'

- an emphasis on customer choice, customer service and consumer rather than provider-led services

- an emphasis on consultation and community involvement (e.g. in community care planning, urban regeneration and Agenda 21)

- the move to unitary authorities in some parts of the country.

They add up to a view of government dominated by market principles, albeit with a strong concern about regulation and audit. But they also add up to a view of local government as one of a number of actors in the locality, with ambivalent views as to what its powers and role in this environment should be – in the UK, the powers of the state have been centralised to a degree unparalleled in most other Western countries (Batley, 1993). The emphasis is on local government as an 'enabling' authority, although the interpretation of enabling varies from a role where the authority simply awards and manages service contracts to one where the authority carries out a lead role in identifying needs and orchestrating local resources. Not all changes have been imposed from the centre. Many authorities, for example, in response to disenchantment with public services, have developed their own decentralised systems of service delivery and some have experimented with devolution of decision-making.

These policies have given voluntary organisations a much greater role in service provision (from the supply of social housing through housing associations to the provision of social care services on contract). They have also increased the number of statutory funders and other agencies to whom voluntary organisations need to relate, and have brought a range of new actors into the not-for-profit territory as, for example, local authorities have 'floated off' housing stock and residential homes in response to new restrictions imposed by central government. They have further given voluntary and community organisations access to planning and decision-making and demanded a responsiveness to users which is characteristic of some, but by no means all, voluntary sector providers.

The voluntary/statutory relationship

The term 'voluntary and community sector' masks considerable diversity – a diversity which many partners find difficult to grasp (Kendall and Knapp, 1995; Roberts et al., 1995). This means that relationships with government vary considerably. Gidron et al. (1992) have identified three functions of the sector: service; social; representational. The voluntary sector may relate to local government as a service provider, as a group of citizens, as an advocate or self-help group channelling user and community views, or as a campaigner. Its organisations may be national, regional or local and their views may be expressed directly or through intermediary bodies. They may or may not have paid staff – indeed the majority of voluntary organisations are almost totally or totally 'volunteer',[2] and many of these have minimal contact with government bodies, although their activities may well be affected by the patterns and levels of welfare provision that government dictates.

In the nineteenth century, the balance between state and voluntarism ran along what Beatrice Webb characterised as 'parallel bars' when the respective spheres of activity were clearly delineated (Brenton, 1985). With the introduction of the welfare state, it became more like an 'extension ladder', where the voluntary sector supplemented and complemented a foundation of state welfare, often with support from the state. Brenton argues that the welfare state released the sector into a new role 'with the emergence of functions unique to it – those of mutual aid, the provision of information and advice and the critical pressure group function' (1985, p. 3). Over the 1980s, Wolch argues (1990), the role of the voluntary sector was contested between central government, which saw it as an agent, and some local authorities, who supported it as an ally in the defence of local government and supported its political as well as service functions. In the 1990s, although there is some variation at local level, it is the former model which seems to have prevailed, with the voluntary sector expected to take a central role as an agent in the delivery of welfare.

There is a sense in which neither local government nor the voluntary sector is a willing partner to this change. Many voluntary organsiations see their autonomy threatened. Some historians would argue that voluntary organisations, despite their apparent independence, have long acted as agents of the state (Owen, 1964; Ware, 1989). But Jane Lewis (1995, p. 6) suggests that the relationship has moved into a new phase:

> *while a commitment to a mixed economy of welfare in which the part played by the state sector is played down is not new, a situation in which the state determines the conditions of provision without taking responsibility is new.*

Meanwhile, for some local authorities, their very *raison d'être* is under attack. Voluntary sector theorists in the US have been increasingly critical of what they see as a 'conflict paradigm' in both theory and policy, which sees the sector as an alternative to the state or as a buffer between the state and the citizen, rather than as a partner in welfare (see, for example, Salamon, 1987; Kramer *et al.*, 1993). It is this paradigm that has characterised welfare reform in the UK, with the voluntary sector first pushed to the margins by the advocates of state welfare and now seen as an alternative to local government by its critics, offering a more responsive and economical channel for welfare provision

(Kramer *et al.*, 1993).[3] This conflict paradigm is not inevitable. In some European countries – Germany and the Netherlands, for example – a more collaborative model has been in operation for many years, with voluntary organisations as the main provider with significant financial support from government and substantial involvement in corporate systems of policy- and decision-making. It remains to be seen whether similar partnerships can be built up in the UK.

The research

Although this review includes research across the spectrum of voluntary sector activity, the majority of the research reviewed here focuses mainly on two fields – social care and urban regeneration. Much of the recent research on relationships between government and the voluntary sector has been in the social care field: Roberts *et al.* (1995) argue that it is in this field that relationships between the sectors are the most developed. Research in this field has been mainly concerned with funding changes and their wider implications, particularly in relation to the introduction of contracts and the contract culture. It includes case study research on the impact of changing government policy on management and role (Kramer *et al.*, 1993; Prins, 1995; Taylor *et al.*, 1995), on funding (Russell *et al.*, 1995), quality (Blackmore *et al.*, 1995), intermediary bodies (Blackmore *et al.*, forthcoming) and on the overall impact of contracts (Lewis, 1993: Lewis *et al.*, 1995, 1996; Harris, 1996), as well as broader studies on the development of a mixed economy (Wistow *et al.*, 1992; Leat, 1993; Craig, 1994). This review also includes some studies of contracting over a wider field (Deakin and Walsh, 1994; Richardson, 1995; Deakin, 1996).

The growing emphasis on community involvement and partnership in urban regeneration policy has also stimulated a range of studies (MacFarlane, 1993; Pinto, 1995; Taylor, 1995; Hastings *et al.*, 1996; Skelcher *et al.*, 1996). Related to this are more specific studies on: the environment (Stoker and Young, 1993; Young, 1994); housing (Reid, 1995; Reid and Iqbal, 1996; Clapham *et al.*, unpublished); and crime prevention (Edwards, 1995; Nellis, 1995). Other studies of partnerships covered here include Roberts *et al.* (1995), Hambleton *et al.* (1995), and Bemrose and MacKeith (1996).

The impact of change: partners in service

How have these changes affected voluntary and community organisations and their contribution to service delivery?

In 1989, Kramer found little concern, among his sample of 20 national social care organisations, about voluntary/statutory relationships or about funding and regulatory matters. This is perhaps not surprising, since Wistow *et al.* (1992) found that, even in 1991, local authorities were only beginning to implement community care reforms – the watershed was in 1993, with the final stage of implementation, including a requirement that 85 per cent of money transferred from the social security budget to local authorities (as lead agencies in community care) be spent on independent provision. Most research suggests that the implementation and impact of the reforms has varied between authorities (Taylor and Lansley, 1992; Deakin, 1996; Bemrose and MacKeith, 1996). Wistow *et al.* (1992) distinguished five early responses among local authorities (floating voters, conscientious objectors, new beginners, incrementalists and proven enthusiasts). With the culmination of the reforms in 1993, some suggest a new realism may have overtaken the floating voters and new beginners (Taylor and Lewis, 1993) and in their 1996 study Bemrose and MacKeith distinguish four approaches (see Figure 1).

Figure 3.1 Local authority responses to change

Four local authority responses to change
• **cautious authorities** (who try to maintain traditional ways of doing things – often traditional Labour authorities)
• **responsive authorities** (which see the disadvantages involved but try to make it work as well as possible for the locality – Wistow *et al.*'s 'incrementalists', perhaps)
• **business authorities** (who have adopted a pragmatic managerialist approach)
• **residual authorities** (who aim to contract everything out in keeping with a narrow definition of an 'enabling role' – tend to be new right Conservative authorities).

Source: adapted from Bemrose and MacKeith, 1996

The issues that these changes raise for the voluntary sector can be grouped under two headings:

- capacity: how equipped are voluntary and community organisations to take on new roles; who are the winners and losers; what are the costs and benefits?

- control: who will determine the future role, shape and operations of voluntary and community organisations?

Capacity

Government funding represents some 40 per cent of total voluntary sector income in the UK (Kendall and Knapp, 1996). If Housing Corporation funding is disregarded, local government emerges as the most significant statutory funder. Indeed, Kendall and Knapp (1996) argue that local government is a primary point of contact for a significant number of voluntary and community organisations. It is difficult to establish an agreed picture on the way funding is being affected over time, however. Statistics show a significant increase in statutory funding in the 1980s as do more focused case studies (Kramer *et al.*, 1993). Studies are now reporting a decline in overall income (Taylor-Gooby, 1994) for the majority of charities. But despite a dip in the late 1980s, local authority spending on the sector is once again rising in real terms and as a proportion of total expenditure (Mocroft, 1994), albeit still very low at 1.5 per cent. Studies which chart funding changes at a local level over time are hard to come by, but Russell *et al.* (1995), most of whose small sample of 17 social care organisations receive more than half of their income from statutory sources, report major increases in funding to these organisations between 1989 and 1995. These increases are greater in some services than others, however. Russell *et al.* (1995) find that organisations serving elderly people were much more likely to benefit from increased income over the 1993/4 period (mainly because of the Special Transitional Grant that accompanied the community care reforms) than those serving children and families. Indeed, Deakin (1996) suggests that the initial monies available through the Special Transitional Grant (STG) 'washed out' initial concerns that the community care reforms would lead to reductions in funding, which are only now beginning to resurface.

Deakin (1996) reports a traditional preference for voluntary organisations among purchasers. They offer a 'halfway house' to purchasing authorities who wish to ensure that providers have a sense of public responsibility (Roberts *et al.*, 1995). Nonetheless, anecdotal evidence at local level suggests considerable pressure on funding. Why the gap between perception and reality? Russell *et al.* (1995) suggest that, even though their funding picture is one of success, there are deep contradictions within it. They paint a picture of insecurity and short-term funds, cross-subsidy and insufficient funding for the task. Other studies add to this list concerns about the impact of the reforms on the human resources available to the sector and about the specific impact of local government reorganisation.

Insecurity

Despite the overall upward trend, 15 of Russell *et al.*'s (1995) 17 case study organisations had experienced a funding decrease in real terms at some time since 1989. Funding was often short-term and put together from a variety of sources, with heavy transaction costs, as organisations juggled a range of funding cycles and demands. Survival, as Roberts *et al.* (1995) confirm, consumes a vast amount of time. But while multiple funding sources can lead to problems, they also grant a measure of independence. Bemrose and MacKeith (1996) note increased security as one of the positives reported by voluntary organisations in their sample. But there is some concern that those organisations who are successful in getting a service agreement to cover most of their funding needs are in danger of becoming too dependent on one source of income (Leat, 1995; Harris, 1996; Commission on the Future of the Voluntary Sector, 1996) and highly vulnerable if the purchaser finds an alternative source of services.

Some of the reasons Russell *et al.* (1995) give for the insecurity attached to funding arise from service agreements and contracts themselves. Deakin (1996) reports the view held by voluntary organisations that purchasers make little allowance for their fragile resource base. Tales of late payment, late decisions, and high transaction costs abound. Deakin and Walsh (1994, p. 11) also find some evidence of funding being cut over the term of community care contracts, while Richardson's study (1995), which covers contracts in all policy fields, suggests that, although a significant minority of respondents had gained greater security from contracting, in about half of the cases, security was undermined by break clauses.

Insecurity also arises from cuts to other agencies on which voluntary organisations depend, in whatever sector. Taylor *et al.* (1995) point out that many services are only viable as part of a network of provision, which may involve all three sectors. The hidden costs of disrupting these networks may be high.

Cross-subsidy
One major issue arising from research into contract funding appears to be the evidence of cross-subsidy (Russell *et al.*, 1995; Bemrose and MacKeith, 1996; Deakin, 1996). For Roberts *et al.* (1995), 'the use of charities as an extension of government' is one of the major concerns arising from their study. Despite many warnings in the practice literature that organisations should be careful to cost out and include all their overheads, it is likely that some costs remain hidden in a competitive environment, while less experienced organisations in particular may overlook essential costs. Richardson (1995) suggests that 53 per cent of respondents had to subsidise their contracts from their own funds. While this may be appropriate if the purchaser's money is a grant to secure existing services, it could be considered less so if it is meant to secure services dictated

by the purchaser. Craig (1994) reports that national charities are no longer prepared to top up payments to residential homes for new clients.

Human resources
Bemrose and MacKeith (1996, p. 38) underline the multiple accountability of the sector, and its importance for the distinctive contribution that voluntary organisations make:

> *Voluntary organisations operate through a delicate balance of interests and motivations of different parties. Insensitive intervention from outside can disrupt the balance with damaging consequences for the organisations and its clients.*

Russell *et al.* (1995) report that their sample organisations expect changes to committee structures, committee membership and employment hierarchies, as a result of contracts and service agreements; a finding reinforced by Harris (1996). They argue that contract negotiations mean that power in some organisations in their sample lies increasingly with one or two committee members and chief officers. Lewis (1993) and Taylor *et al.* (1995) report cases where existing volunteers and volunteer managers felt squeezed out or alienated by the new contract culture, while Harris (1993) and Bemrose and MacKeith (1996) report difficulties in recruitment. The need for tightly regulated services may sit uneasily with the use of volunteers. There is also some limited evidence in Taylor *et al.* (1995) that support in kind from government employees and in the form of buildings and equipment may be threatened by tighter costing procedures in government. How broadly these experiences are shared remains to be established, however. Richardson's NCVO study (1995) reports no evidence of volunteers withdrawing because of the pressures of contracting.

What gets funded: lack of core funding
Cross-subsidy comes perilously close to dumping, and research on estate regeneration underlines the need to ensure that resident organisations managing services need resources adequate to the task (Taylor, 1995). Particularly important in this respect is the provision of core and development funds. This development funding is available for the development of tenant management organisations, but not in other fields. This is a particular disadvantage for smaller organisations who have no reserves and cannot carry additional costs or who do not feel they have the skills to provide services on contract. Such organisations might normally look to a local council for voluntary service or similar body for support. This voluntary sector infrastructure, through its training and information, can make the difference between survival and demise for smaller organisations who do not have the capacity to buy in expertise and

do not have access to national umbrella bodies. Evidence from Blackmore *et al.* (forthcoming), however, suggests that intermediary bodies in some areas (e.g. rural areas) may themselves be drawn into direct service provision. Sometimes they are the only organisation with the capacity to respond to market opportunities. At other times, direct service provision may be the only way they can survive financially (Newcastle Architecture Workshop, 1990). This raises serious dilemmas about the compatibility of service, development and representational roles as well as the possibility of competition with member organisations.

What gets funded: potential loss of complementary role

Voluntary organisations have traditionally offered services that are complementary to mainstream provision. Researchers fear that funding will dry up for groups who do not deliver the services that are now a priority for purchasing or that organisations providing much needed complementary services may be seduced away from their original goals by new opportunities (Bemrose and MacKeith, 1996). Although the Commission on the Future of the Voluntary Sector (1996, p. 54) cites a commitment from the Association of Directors of Social Services to the support of 'organisations concerned with community action, advocacy and voluntary activity', this is uneven at local level. Some studies report authorities or areas who have moved to contracts for all services and abandoned grant-aid, or retained only a reduced grant-aid budget for very small one-off grants (Blackmore *et al.*, 1995; Russell *et al.*, 1995). Although some studies still find evidence of money for user advocacy (Taylor *et al.*, 1995; Blackmore *et al.*, forthcoming), Kendall and Knapp (1996) suggest that funds for advice, self-help and cultural activities have not been maintained, a finding reinforced in Taylor-Gooby's study (1994). The absorption of the Urban Programme into the Single Regeneration Budget (SRB) leaves few alternative sources of funds for community groups who are not tied into partnerships (see also Taylor, 1995). Bemrose and MacKeith (1996) argue for the importance of maintaining a range of funding mechanisms within government. If this does not happen, many of the 'complementary' roles of voluntary organisations will be at risk – the safety nets and support systems on which mainstream services rely and without which the demand for mainstream services can be expected to increase. Kendall and Knapp (1996) argue that a balance between contractual and non-contractual funding is essential to the development of a balanced relationship between the voluntary sector and the state, but that non-contractual funding comes mostly from local government and is a 'soft target' in times of financial retrenchment. They suggest that black and ethnic minority groups are particularly at risk, since they are often funded on 'soft' money and their holistic approach is less amenable to contracts.

Who wins?

There are different views on the extent of contracting. But Kendall and Knapp (1996) comment that the move from grants to contracts may in the end be less threatening than the promotion of competitive tendering (and, we might add, other competitive funds like the Single Regeneration Budget Challenge Fund). Most studies agree that contracts are most likely to go to known and trusted organisations, to favour the larger household name charities and those who are most active in local networks. They are more likely to have the relevant expertise on tap: 'in the performance culture of the mid-1990s, visible success or lack of it can be self-perpetuating ' (Russell *et al.*, unpublished).

While early DoH guidance (and the White Paper, *Caring for People*) positively encouraged market and community development, there is evidence that these development roles have been overtaken by more pressing imperatives, not least the need to deliver services at the lowest cost (Lewis *et al.*, 1995). The absence of a market development role is seen by researchers to present a particular threat to smaller organisations, who do not have the resources to bear the considerable transactions costs attached to contracting (Bemrose and MacKeith, 1996; Russell *et al.*, 1995; Taylor *et al.*, 1995). It is also a major problem in rural areas, where the voluntary sector is often poorly developed. Chanan (1991) has for some time been drawing attention to the difficulties facing smaller organisations across a wide spectrum and the lack of recognition of their considerable contribution. A similar concern for development is expressed in the urban regeneration literature (Taylor, 1995), where tenant management of services or community involvement in larger-scale partnerships depends crucially on the experience and capacity built through traditions of smaller-scale activity. Community and voluntary sector involvement in Challenge Fund bids was disappointingly low during the first round (Clarke, G., 1995). Smaller organisations are also disadvantaged by the inadequate information base on which local authorities work. Russell *et al.* (1995), Taylor *et al.* (1995) and Bemrose and MacKeith (1996) all underline the need for local authorities to be better informed, while acknowledging the difficulties involved in mapping a diverse and shifting population (Shore *et al.*, 1994).

Hoyes *et al.* (1993) argue that decentralised purchaser structures are likely to benefit smaller local organisations, and it is also possible that 'spot' rather than 'block' purchase could favour such organisations, although the latter offers a precarious basis on which to plan (Bemrose and MacKeith, 1996). For black and ethnic minority groups, contracts may offer a more open and fair system to gain access to funders – one that is less open to patronage and less locked into the past (Craig, 1994) – although there is little evidence as yet to support or deny this.

Local government reorganisation

The unexploded time bomb in relation to funding is local government reorganisation. There is little information on the current situation (although NCVO did monitor the situation in the early stages), but the experience of the abolition of the metropolitan counties does not give cause for optimism, especially as there is unlikely to be an equivalent of the London Boroughs Grant Committee to pick up the many pieces that are likely to slip between the cracks of reorganisation. Craig (1994) suggests that authorities outside the main centres of population tend to see the voluntary sector as the 'volunteer' sector and that voluntary sector budgets will be particularly hard hit in these areas. He suggests that the reduction in size of social services departments will put at risk funding of user participation and carers' services. Organisations covering areas that cross the new boundaries are also likely to be in difficulties. Mercer (1995) points out that some organisations may need to make legal changes where assets straddle new administrative boundaries. Ethnic minority groups are again likely to be particularly hard hit, especially in areas where there are low numbers. There is an urgent need to monitor this situation and establish a baseline on which to assess the overall impact. Improving statistical information on the voluntary sector will assist with this, but needs to be backed up with qualitative information.

The positives of partnership

The picture is not all one of gloom. The 85 per cent rule in the Special Transitional Grant has also, as Russell et al. (1995) show, provided significant opportunities for growth in community care. The Commission on the Future of the Voluntary Sector (1996) reports an 'overall change in the attitude of local government towards voluntary action, modifying earlier scepticism about the motivation and capacities of voluntary bodies'. The Single Regeneration Budgets, with its emphasis on partnership, does have the potential to fund a range of community-based activities in areas with successful bids, as did City Challenge (MacFarlane, 1993). It also offers opportunities beyond the Urban Programme localities. There are other fields where money is being made available, either through central government programmes or through new local authority initiatives to fund local voluntary organisations. In the environmental field, for example, Young (1994) reports a surge of interest from 'third force organisations' in carrying out projects in partnership with local authorities and vice versa, while Nellis (1995) suggests that voluntary organisations and local authorities have long been allies in the search for new approaches to criminal justice and have been able to use Safer Cities money to good effect (although this programme has had limited geographical coverage).

Moves towards user- and community-managed services are also a considerable step forward. Clapham *et al.*'s unpublished research on community-based housing co-operatives suggests that 'small, locally-based and resident-controlled housing organisations can provide an effective service and, crucially, can sustain this over a considerable period of time.' However, researchers in the field of urban regeneration are critical of the pressure that cuts in services – and care in the community policies – place on community-based organisations and informal systems in stressed communities. They argue that, while the opportunity to manage services should be made widely available, the level of involvement in management should remain open to choice and that community management should not be allowed to displace or discourage advocacy and representative functions (Taylor, 1995).

Control: partner or agent?

Voluntary organisations are supposed to bring to welfare the virtues of flexibility, responsiveness to need, ability to innovate and ability to harness charitable resources and voluntary activity. But there are widespread fears that the tighter accountability that contracts bring and a preoccupation with value for money will prejudice these qualities. How justified are the fears that many voluntary organisations have expressed, i.e. that the 'contract culture' will distort the mission and the operating cultures of voluntary organisations and turn them into mere agents (see, for example, Gutch, 1992)?

Role

In his 1989 fieldwork in the UK, Kramer found little evidence that government funding, a significant source in his study, had distorted the mission of the agencies he studied or even affected their advocacy role (Kramer *et al.*, 1993). Would this still be the case in 1995?

The NCVO survey on the impact of contracts (Richardson, 1995) finds little evidence that the operation of contracts is distorting the objectives of voluntary sector contractors. However, there is some evidence that organisations are changing direction in order to chase new money. Russell *et al.* (1995) report also that in some instances, process goals have been squeezed out, as in the case of a child care organisation which trained local women as part of its aims, but found the conditions of the contract made this difficult.

One respect in which Richardson's survey does find evidence of change of direction is in relation to client groups and geographical coverage. Voluntary sector providers find themselves under some pressure to serve clients referred by statutory services, rather than the clients they served as complementary providers (see also Taylor *et al.*, 1995; Bemrose and MacKeith, 1996). It could be argued, for example, that housing associations have already seen their clientele increasingly dictated by government imperatives, as the capacity of local authorities is diminished (Page, 1994). This change in coverage could put at risk the preventative role that voluntary organisations have played in serving those not yet in 'high risk' categories, if contracts and service agreements replace grant-aid. Contracts and service agreements are also more likely to be confined to the purchaser's geographical area, a change which is likely to be exacerbated by the move to smaller unitary authorities, and which again has the potential of leaving existing voluntary sector clients without a service in the future.

Lewis (1993) suggests that there are tensions between advocacy and service delivery, a concern also raised by voluntary organisations in Deakin's study (1996). Organisations may not find delivering mainstream services compatible with an advocacy role, they may be discouraged by purchasers, or they may be considered to have vested interests. At a more practical level, Lewis reports that the administration of a contract in one of her case studies simply left no time for advocacy. Barnes *et al.* (1994) also report a tension between service and advocacy among user groups. However, Richardson's 1995 survey finds no evidence of a reduction in advocacy and campaigning activity.

The shape of the sector
Distortion can occur at the level of the individual organisation or at the level of the sector as a whole. If the market ceases to support objectives which are not priorities for purchasers, then the shape of the sector may alter past recognition.

Several studies note the growth of a new not-for-profit sector which appears to have little in common with the rest of the voluntary sector – floated-off trusts, new professional partnerships, the increasing number of housing associations who see themselves as part of the private sector (Reid, 1995; Taylor *et al.*, 1995). Craig (1994) found that one in four authorities in his study had established independent trusts. Whether these new bodies contribute to more choice and diversity within the sector has yet to be tested. But they are likely to be advantaged in the market, because of their size, expertise, networks and above all their knowledge of the purchaser. A parallel development (Blackmore *et al.*, forthcoming), which raises further questions about the shape, character and accountability of the sector, is the separation of charitable companies from the rest of the organisation in agencies where large contracts are being taken on, in order to protect trustees.

These developments raise questions as to whether it is meaningful any more to talk about a 'voluntary sector', whether that matters and what it is that is being created instead. If the voluntary sector is expected to bring distinctive characteristics into welfare, then the type of organisation that is 'trading' under these auspices is of concern, especially if there are tax benefits involved or other kinds of preferential treatment. Some commentators predict a split within the voluntary sector between large not-for-profit organisations which are closer to either the statutory or business sector in culture and operation and small grass-roots organisations (Knight, 1993; Russell *et al.*, 1995), arguing in Knight's case that tax advantages should no longer accrue to the former. While this is oversimplistic, it does place an obligation on those who claim special privileges for the sector to define what it is that is valuable and distinctive about the organisations operating within it and how this can be guaranteed. If the term becomes a flag of convenience, then it will cease to have any value. The changing shape of the sector also matters to local authorities in so far as they are responsible for the overall pattern of provision that exists in their areas. If purchasing policies squeeze out a whole range of complementary activities, as indicated above, patterns of provision will be the poorer for it.

Operations
As the role of the local government funder moves from investor to purchaser, the nature of the relationship is likely to change. What does this mean for the kinds of service that the local authority 'enables'?

Fears of over-regulation have been common from the outset of contracting. Where responsibility for services is decentralised,

> *regulation and inspection, published performance indicators ... and a battery of incentives are among the means that the centre has used to keep a grip on events.* (Deakin and Walsh, 1994, p. 5)

This is a story that local authorities will recognise from their own relationship with central government. But often these accountability requirements are passed on further down the line and further magnified (Leat, 1988). This is exacerbated by the considerable scepticism that local authorities still have about the management capacity of voluntary organisations, especially smaller ones (Deakin, 1996) and the resistance of some to what they see as an attack on their own services. It is also exacerbated by the difficulty of measuring many of the activities which are purchased from voluntary organisations. The tendency in these circumstances to fall back on crude financial measures is well-documented in the wider organisational literature (see, for example, Scott and Meyer, 1993) and fails to capitalise on the energy that some in the sector have given to developing appropriate forms of monitoring and evaluation (Young, 1991).

Nonetheless, we should be wary of smoke without fire. Kramer (1994) argues that: 'There is a tendency among voluntary sector leaders in England and elsewhere to exaggerate somewhat the effects of government funding on bureaucratisation'. It is also possible that the conditions that prevailed before the supposed advent of the 'contract culture' are viewed through rose-coloured spectacles. Contracts existed prior to the 1990s and complaints about inappropriate monitoring were heard about grant regimes. Both the Manpower Services Commission programmes of the 1980s and the Urban Programme had tight monitoring regimes. So what is the evidence so far?

NCVO, after expressing considerable reservations about the move towards contracts, is now reporting that early fears of interference in operational matters may have been exaggerated, especially since the majority of organisations in their survey (Richardson, 1995) were involved in writing the service specification. Deakin (1996) reports considerable variation along a spectrum from loose and trusting to tight contracts and suggests that contracts with voluntary organisations fall on the less-precise side of the line. Walsh (1995) claims that voluntary organisations do feel their flexibility is being reduced. But some of the pressure for clarity is coming from providers themselves: Richardson (1995) and others report that voluntary organisations see greater clarity as one of the benefits of contracts, while Bemrose and MacKeith (1996) list security, clarity and equal status offered by contracts as the advantages from a voluntary sector point of view.

However, Bemrose and MacKeith (1996) suggest that contracts are being used where grants would be more appropriate. They also report (1996, p. 10) that some voluntary organisations in their sample feel that their independence and flexibility, their capacities for innovation and their personal touch can be compromised by contracts. The move to contracts is often accompanied by a change in personnel, as voluntary sector liaison officers with in-depth knowledge of the service area are replaced by contract officers which a much more confined perspective (see also Taylor and Lewis, 1993). There are early examples of quite inappropriate contract specifications (Taylor and Lewis, 1993; *NCVO News,* 1993, p. 8). Richardson (1995) refers to local authorities where there is still considerable interference in the delivery of a contract and also reports that organisations serving unpopular causes feel especially pressured. Birchall *et al.* (1995) comment on the considerable centralisation in the new-style service delivery agencies they studied (including NHS trusts, grant-maintained schools and voluntary housing transfers) and the Commission on the Future of the Voluntary Sector (1996) reports voluntary sector concern with 'excessive bureaucracy'. Blackmore *et al.* (1995) expose the enormous gap between rhetoric and practice, contrasting a general statement by the local authority associations about not being too prescriptive with their suggested guidelines on day care specifications which run to 20 sections and 21 pages. Several studies underline the considerable time and costs involved in both negotiating contracts and in contract review, even when small amounts of money are involved (Russell *et al.*, 1995; Lewis, 1993), while others underline the problems caused by inconsistent policies across local authority departments.

This raises the further question of accountability. Kendall and Knapp (1996) argue that 'accountability to government or its agents is a logical corollary of government funding and is one of the biggest issues facing the sector today. ' Indeed, some researchers point to the problems caused by the attenuation of state accountability, e.g. in housing associations (Riseborough, 1995). Most voluntary organisations welcome moves to better management and accountability, but this does not make accountability simple. As Kendall and Knapp (1996) argue, accountability mechanisms can 'drive a wedge between helper and helped when many organisations are trying hard not to make this distinction'. Furthermore, chains of accountability are attenuated by the contracting process and Blackmore *et al.* (1995) argue that more attention needs to be given to the question of where responsibility and accountability should lie. Following Leat's (1988) seminal work on this subject, there has been little research interest in accountability, although there is growing interest in the associated area of quality assurance (Blackmore *et al.*, 1995).

The transaction costs involved in monitoring, regulation and accountability can be high for both sides, but especially for smaller organisations and those with little or no core capacity. Taylor *et al.* (1995) underline the disadvantage faced by smaller and community-based organisations in adhering to complex training and regulation requirements and argue the need to explore different regulation requirements according to size and user preference. They suggest (1995, p. 65) that:

> *some of the resources that are now going into regulatory structures could usefully be diverted into support for user- and carer-based organisations to help them define the standards and quality of the support they need.*

It is important to recognise that, while there are undoubted cases of over-regulation, many voluntary organisations would support the need to ensure safety and quality. There is an inevitable tension between the need for regulation and safety on the one hand and the flexibility and consumer responsiveness that voluntary organisations are supposed to provide on the other, which is not easy to resolve. It is also dangerous to assume that the power always lies with the purchaser. As a tradition of 'third-party' government builds up, the critical mass of professional expertise which remains with local government is likely to dissipate and purchasers may be much more dependent on the information supplied by ever more powerful providers. US research suggests that, in a sellers' market, voluntary organisations can exert considerable influence in negotiations on contracts and service agreements (Kramer, 1994), although Russell *et al.* (1995) suggest that this applies more to large, national organisations than to small community-based ones. Blackmore *et al.* (forthcoming) echo US findings that successful bidders are unlikely to lose contracts once allocated, although Taylor and Lewis (1993) and Deakin and Walsh (1994) find evidence of contracts being renegotiated before time and to the disadvantage of contractors.

The pressure for growth and formalisation that comes with contracts may be appropriate for the service the purchaser requires but not for the provider. Prins (1995) describes the way in which small, unambitious volunteer-run organisations find they are turning into different animals: 'Many of the organisations in the study had begun as sole providers of a fairly light or recreational service; they are now providers of a primary and fairly intensive service.' She argues that the very advantages that make these small organisations attractive to policy-makers and purchasers may be related to the limited nature of the original service and be an impediment to the provision of a 'core, intensive and accountable service'. Both Bemrose and MacKeith (1996) and Russell *et al.* (1995) report the pressure on voluntary organisations to grow, but while purchase of service undoubtedly contributes to that pressure, Taylor *et al.* (1995) point out that there are other factors outside the voluntary/statutory relationship which encourage growth and formalisation. While the consequences of growth need to be addressed if the diversity of the sector is to be maintained, the answer does not lie solely with purchasers of voluntary sector services.

Voluntary organisations in the University of Birmingham study felt that contracting had brought few gains for users (Walsh, 1995). Services managed by or in partnership with users may overcome this problem (Walsh, 1995, p. 11), but even in successful community-based housing associations, models are still imposed from outside, with limited potential for direct democracy (Clapham *et al.*, unpublished): 'The power of the community is limited through the rules of the game and the difficulties in marshalling appropriate resources to play the game.'

Studies on housing estates show that outside professionals can still exert considerable influence over community-managed services and enterprises (Taylor, 1995), even if they are only observers. Urban regeneration experience suggests in any case that there is a tension between managing services and representing community interests. It may be that parallel representative structures are needed to hold community-managed services to account (Gibson, 1993; Hastings *et al.*, 1996).

Harris (1996) reports a disturbing gap between purchaser perceptions of the contracting process and provider perceptions, a gap which is also evident in the findings of the University of Birmingham research (Walsh, 1995; Deakin, 1996). A number of researchers have commented that the new management in local authorities seems some way behind leading-edge thinking in business (Leat, 1993; Taylor *et al.*, 1995). J. Clarke (1995) has argued that post-Fordism in public management seems to have been accompanied by many of the management premises of Fordism. Given that some of the language used by leading thinkers in business has a strong resonance in the voluntary and community sectors, there is surely scope for a two-way traffic in management thinking. There is a need to develop new experiments which draw on the best of business thinking and apply it to change in the voluntary sector and to relationships with suppliers (Taylor and Hoggett, 1994). This resonates with the call in Taylor *et al.*'s 1995 research for experimentation in new organisational forms which allow organisations the chance to stay small and yet benefit from economies of scale (see also Houghton and Timperley, 1992; Norton, 1995).

Summary

It is too early to make confident conclusions about the impact of the move to the market and the increasing use of contracts on the voluntary sector. Even if clear messages emerged from the findings so far, we are in a stage of rapid transition which may not predict accurately what will happen in the longer term. Local authorities, as well as voluntary organisations, are learning 'on the run'. Deakin (1996) is among many who conclude that the worst fears have not been realised. It may, he argues, be 'a small revolution – not many dead' (Deakin, 1996, p. 24). But he argues that there is little evidence as yet that the revolution is benefiting the service users who are still marginal to much of the current policy debate, despite the rhetoric.

There are many tensions still to be resolved if the revolution is to be a peaceful and productive one. Drawing on Bemrose and MacKeith (1996) it is possible to identify three such tensions: between the local authority need to contract out and the distinctive mission that many voluntary organisations were set up to fulfil (which threatens the shape of the sector); between the need for responsible control on the purchaser's part and flexibility on the part of the provider (which threaten the operating strengths associated with the sector); between the local authority's necessary concern with equality and overview and the particular concerns of voluntary organisations, which reminds us that the goals and motivations of voluntary organisations are fundamentally different from those of the state. If these tensions are to be resolved or at least confronted (there may be no resolution as such), the evident gulf in perceptions between statutory purchasers and voluntary sector organisations (Harris, 1996) will need to be bridged. This is a concern to which we shall return in the next section.

Partners in policy

The changes

Public participation in service and area planning is nothing new. But new requirements have come from central government legislation over recent years requiring consultation with voluntary, community and service user organisations and most recently in local Agenda 21 discussions. There are many incentives to partnership for local authorities. While money is one of these, others include: the focusing of resources, the synergy that comes from pooling different energies and the likelihood that residents will ensure that changes which they have helped plan will be maintained in the long term (Hastings *et al.*, 1996). A concept of the 'enabling authority' is required that goes far beyond purchasing in the market place to encouraging and orchestrating the activities of a wide range of local actors and resources to common ends (Stewart and Taylor, 1993; Stewart and Stoker, 1995). These developments take their place in a wider 'revolution', as networks and alliances replace traditional hierarchical patterns of delivery and decision-making and 'policy making is increasingly dependent on securing the collaboration of, and between, groups of diverse organisations' (Reid, 1995, p. 133). As Pinto (1995) argues, 'simply doing things as before is not an option'.

Several commentators see a crucial role for voluntary and community organisations in bringing different interests into public debate and especially those of the most excluded in society. Nellis (1995, p. 103) argues that being responsive to communities 'is the cornerstone of the Probation Service's survival as a welfare agency' and 'has the potential to transform the very nature of the organisation'. The same is true of local government. Local government commentators have laid increasing emphasis on notions of community governance and citizen empowerment: the need, as Wahlberg *et al.* (1995) put it, 'for the state to belong to local society rather than the other way round'. If this is the rhetoric, what is the reality? Research suggests there is considerable variation across the country, between service areas and between local authorities. Four main themes emerge from the growing body of work on partnerships and joint planning. These are: the impact of central government policy; local capacity; competition; and power.

National policy

Central government resources or directives have been an important trigger for partnership and the involvement of voluntary, community and user organisations. But there are tensions between this involvement and other policies emanating from central government. Skelcher *et al.* (1996) note the absence of engagement from the centre in partnerships. Central government is the ghost at the feast, as it were, setting agendas but not open to influence. In the urban regeneration field, researchers have been particularly critical of the unrealistic timescales attached to bidding processes (Estate Action, City Challenge, Scottish Partnerships, and now the Single Regeneration Budget Challenge Fund) (Taylor, 1995; Hastings *et al.*, 1996; Skelcher *et al.*, 1996). These have not allowed time for communities to develop the capacity to engage as partners. Nor does funding based on tightly predicted outcomes allow the flexibility for communities to develop their contribution as programmes progress.

Research on urban regeneration suggests that multi-agency working is beset with problems but, here too, the difficulties are exacerbated by the lack of co-ordination between government departments, with policies from one cutting across policies from another. Central government's regional offices are beginning to address this issue, but Hastings *et al.* (1996) comment on the benefits of the Welsh and Scottish offices, where all central government functions are represented.

On the other hand, both Scotland and Wales are in the throes of major local government reorganisations, as are some English authorities. Hambleton *et al.* (1995) and McCabe *et al.* (1994) underline the problems that local government reorganisation may cause for voluntary and community organisations, as key contacts change and planning blight descends. Organisational structures designed for existing systems will need to be redesigned; separate campaigns for change will have to be fought across an increasing number of fronts; the joint boards which many commentators envisage will be more difficult to approach and influence. However, Mercer (1995) suggests that unitary authorities may offer a better fit with the more holistic ways of working in the voluntary and community sectors than two-tier systems based on a functional split.

Research suggests that continuity is essential to effective networks and is generally critical of the cascade of change in local authorities that central government policies have caused, with its potential to disrupt relationships (although it can also open up new connections). Increasing fragmentation of service providers can be a particular problem for locally based organisations. McCabe *et al.* (1994), for example, underline the difficulties of negotiating with each individual school rather than the education authority. The proliferation of partnership boards, co-ordinating bodies and other joint ventures required of today's service environment can itself be bewildering to negotiate and add to a confusing overall picture.

Capacity

Wistow *et al.* (1992, p. 33) argue that voluntary organisations have long been embedded in the policy process, through 'complex interweaving of elected members and management boards', a point reinforced by an Association of District Councils publication (1992). They and others suggest, however, that this is more likely to be true of the larger organisations,[4] and that, when it comes to new networking arrangements, such organisations hold the advantage, in terms both of access and influence. They are known; they have more time and resources and more political experience; they may be monopoly providers. They are also more likely to be able to hold their own. Where smaller organisations are involved, they can be seen as more malleable and easily incorporated (Reid and Iqbal, 1996).

Russell *et al.* (1995) and Skelcher *et al.* (1996) find that smaller organisations are simply less likely to be on important networks – as are black and ethnic minority groups. The experience of the Single Regeneration Budget Challenge Fund suggests that voluntary organisations or councils for voluntary service are often consulted by partnerships as a proxy for communities (Clarke, G., 1995). It is difficult for smaller organisations with few resources to redress this imbalance. Many community-based organisations are unfamiliar with the cultures of decision-making in which they are expected to participate. Even those who are in demand face difficult choices, as many in black and ethnic minority organisations have discovered. Small organisations may simply not have the personnel to service a proliferation of consultative and partnership systems. Time spent in servicing networks is time out of the front-line and away from those for whom the organisation was set up. Even if this can be justified, they have to ask whether the opportunity cost is worth it.

Research repeatedly emphasises the time that is needed to allow community and voluntary organisations to build their individual and organisational capacity. Partnership does not only require time and skills of individual organisations, however. It requires an infrastructure to open up opportunities, provide information and link networks together (Skelcher *et al.*, 1996). The voluntary sector infrastructure in this country has a long tradition and is well-developed in most localities. But surprisingly little is known about the different patterns of co-ordination in different localities and different parts of the sector and a previous section of this paper has already underlined its extreme vulnerability in the current funding climate.

Councils for voluntary service and similar bodies can give professional help, but Hastings *et al.* (1996) also underline the importance of community umbrella bodies as a channel for representation if smaller, community-based organisations are to have influence. Roberts *et al.* (1995) reinforce this argument but emphasise the difficulty that many organisations face in finding structures that can have the confidence both of their diverse communities and their partners. Much more research is needed on the advantages and disadvantages of different models, both for communities themselves and the wider partnership. Hastings *et al.* (1996) outline some of the models available (see also MacFarlane, 1993). But there are no blueprints, and Roberts *et al.* (1995) warn local authorities against 'municipalising' infrastructure provision for the voluntary or community sectors – a temptation increased by the requirements for community involvement against tight timescales in government funding programmes.

Hastings *et al.* (1996) demonstrate how fragile apparently robust community structures can be. New demands for partnership put heavy pressure on existing support and representative structures and networks, and have in some cases led to a fundamental overhaul. Communities cannot be expected to make a full input to partnership when they are also trying to get the appropriate machinery into place and working. Funding programmes which do not recognise the need for flexibility over time, therefore, disempower communities further.

Partnership requires capacity not only in the voluntary sector but also in the local authority. Skelcher *et al.* (1996) underline the importance of 'champions' at a high level in local authorities if partnership is to work. But even with considerable commitment, partnership is not easy. Skelcher *et al.* (1996, p. 22) point out that 'few individuals, if any, are paid to engage in networking and it is not normally seen as a specific organisational objective'. Many studies also underline the importance of training in the community and in authorities if partnership is to be effective.

Competition
An increasingly competitive funding environment creates tensions for co-operation at all levels: within and between authorities, between authorities and the voluntary sector and between voluntary organisations. Hunter (1992) has argued that increased competition militates against the trust necessary to develop the seamless service that is part of current rhetoric. People protect their expertise because it now represents their capital; they are not sure how much information to share with an agency that might be a competitor (Skelcher *et al.*, 1996).

Edwards (1994) comments that rivalries between agencies have long been a feature of British government. Local voluntary and community sector partners tend to get sidelined on the margins of the wheeling and dealing between 'official agencies'. In community care, it is the evolving relationship between local and health authorities which will be key to decision-making networks and the place of voluntary organisations within them.

The 'conflict paradigm' which views voluntary organisations as an alternative to the state has militated against co-operative relationships between the two, at least in 'cautious' authorities, protective of their service tradition. Market principles, rigorously interpreted, have also led in some cases to the exclusion of voluntary sector providers from joint planning, because they are seen to have a vested interest in the placement of contracts. Although Wistow *et al.* (1992) argue that providers, whether in or outside the local authority, can be closer to consumer needs than purchasers, local authorities who now see themselves as the real representatives of consumers as well as citizens may fail to consider the other qualities that voluntary organisations may bring to the planning process.

Power
Research to date suggests that, while *access* to policy networks may have improved, the *influence* of voluntary and community organisations remains that of the 'peripheral insider' (Maloney *et al.*, 1994). Hastings *et al.* (1996) report that community representatives have had a modest impact on partnerships, mainly at the implementation stage (a finding reinforced by both MacFarlane, 1993 and Skelcher *et al.*, 1996). Even that depends very much on the issue (social and housing issues are more amenable to community influence than economic and employment issues). In a classic illustration of Lukes's[5] analysis of power,

community issues rarely get onto the agenda and community representatives declare themselves satisfied with achievements which in no way match up to the rhetoric of partnership (Stewart and Taylor, 1996). Hastings *et al.* (1996) describe what is going on in the ten partnerships they have studied as 'quality consultation'. This is a considerable improvement on previous exercises, but falls far short of the rhetoric of partnership and community government. They question whether this level of impact is a sufficient reward for the energy and resources that residents put into the process, and ask whether involvement in partnership simply removes the cutting edge of communities.

As Reid and Iqbal (1996) remind us, organisations enter into inter-organisational relations possessing unequal powers and liabilities. In their study of partnerships, Roberts *et al.* (1995) point out that relationships between local voluntary organisations and local authorities are dominated by resource questions. Russell *et al.* (1995) argue further that relationships in community care are distorted by a 'resource lopsidedness' between authorities on the one hand that spend a maximum of 2 to 3 per cent of their budgets on the voluntary sector and voluntary organisations on the other that are dependent on the authority for up to 60 per cent of their income. This not only colours funding negotiations. It is likely to have a knock-on effect on all other negotiations.

Hambleton *et al.* (1995) are among several researchers who comment on the major cultural differences between prospective partners. Much of the work on urban regeneration suggests that it is usually the community that has to adjust to the local authority rather than vice versa (Hastings *et al.*, 1995; Skelcher *et al.*, 1996). Whatever power local authorities feel they have lost, they are still seen as powerful by outsiders (McCabe *et al.*, 1994). Roberts *et al.* (1995) describe the unfair 'rules of engagement' which still characterise partnership and disadvantage community and voluntary sector partners: a major imbalance of confidence, resources and professional expertise; the impermeability of processes and professions; the nature and tone of the dialogue; meeting times and access; and so on. These either keep voluntary and community partners on the margins or co-opt them into decisions and dominant ways of operating that are not their own (Hastings *et al.*, 1996).

If these are the outward and visible factors which prevent partnership, there are more subtle processes at work. One is the informal 'behind-the-scenes' nature of much decision-making. Too often a partnership board is simply a ratifying body. Community representatives find that the real decisions are taken elsewhere. Skelcher *et al.* (1996) distinguish between 'inner and outer networks' arguing that urban regeneration partnerships have enabled community directors on partnership boards to gain access to inner networks. But Kendall and 6 (1994) argue that voluntary organisations lack the resources and *locus standi* to be present in the intensive, regular contact points by which policy communities are knitted together, although as providers they may become more active in producer and professional networks. Reid and Iqbal (1995) distinguish between two network 'cultures' (see Figure 2). The more informal, 'competitive' networks are flexible and confer a lot of autonomy on members. They are entrepreneurial and opportunistic. But they are also the more exclusive, relying on 'organisations using their skills in managing interorganisational relationships to secure their own entry' (Reid and Iqbal, 1995, p. 31). This excludes smaller organisations and user organisations (the latter do not, in any case, fit the 'culture'). The more formal 'collaborative' networks are less exclusive, more concerned with legitimacy, but are also less entrepreneurial and appear to achieve a great deal less than the effort expended by participants. This distinction may explain the lack of power felt by many voluntary, community and user organisations who add legitimacy to formal partnerships, but are excluded from the more entrepreneurial networks where the 'real action' is.

Figure 3.2   Inter-organisational cultures

Competitive	Collaborative
'Can Do'	Developmental
Flexible	Stable
Autonomous	Participative
Opportunistic	High control
Entrepreneurial	Trust-based
Power relationships not fixed	Power fixed
Selective	Inclusive
Output oriented	Process oriented

Source: adapted from Reid and Iqbal, 1996

Two further problems flow from this. Hastings *et al.* (1996) comment on the culture of consensus in which many voluntary and community organisations find themselves. Conflict and dissent are viewed as counterproductive and a smooth process a sign of success. Yet Hastings *et al.* suggest that too smooth a process is a sign that the community partner is weak and the partnership board merely a rubber stamp; they see conflict as a sign that a partnership is healthy. Secondly, as Skelcher *et al.* (1996) point out, partnership processes allow little room for the consultation with users and their public that often characterises voluntary and community sector participants. In these circumstances, co-option into the agendas of partners is an ever-present danger.

A third problem is the thorny issue of representation. A number of studies agree (see, for example, Taylor, 1995; Hastings *et al.*, 1996) that the issue of representation tends to be used as an excuse for not responding to community input by partners whose own representativeness is itself open to question. Community representation is a poisoned chalice.[6] Community representatives are rarely given the resources to inform and be fully informed by their public. Partners fail to recognise the diversity and complexity within communities and have unrealistic expectations of what community representatives can deliver. Yet Hastings *et al.* (1996) suggest that there is something to be said for working with the people who are prepared to put their time and energy into the process and supporting them in ensuring that their input is fully informed by their constituency. In a similar argument, Hambleton *et al.* (1995, p. 62) distinguish between the public at large and the 'interested public':

> *It is clearly the interested public that has provided energy and impetus for innovations in community care. It may be that those concerned with inter-agency working should focus their attention on the interested public if they wish to strengthen the citizen's voice in decision making.*

The positives of partnership

This section has suggested that there is a long way to go before partnership becomes a reality. Despite these reservations, however, it would be foolish to dismiss the achievements and potential of partnership. Community involvement has been given a much higher profile by central government policies. Hastings *et al.* (1996) argue that partnerships have raised organisational and individual capacity in the communities they studied and have established a positive experience and image on which to build. MacFarlane (1993) argues that City Challenge offered many people in the successful areas the opportunity to become involved in implementing projects of their choice. He argues that this involvement in action has as important a contribution to make to participation as being involved in meetings and strategic decision-making (see also Stoker and Young, 1993). Roberts *et al.* (1995) report on a partnership in Birmingham where the initially low-profile housing and social elements in which the community had engaged proved to be the saving grace of a construction-led programme which fell victim to the recession. They describe successful partnerships where local authority and voluntary/community sector interests have combined to extract the maximum public and social good from the minimum local financial investment.

Partnerships seem to work relatively well in policy areas where the local authority has neither competence nor a tradition of service provision but the potential to bring agencies and communities together around issues which belong to everyone and no-one. Crime prevention and environmental issues are two examples in the literature reviewed; health and the various forays into 'quango-watching' might offer similar opportunities (Martin *et al.*, 1995).

Recommendations on the operation of partnerships from research studies include the need for: clear and agreed goals and objectives; time; continuity and stability; commitment throughout partner organisations (i.e. vertical as well as horizontal); adequate resources for community partners; results; and a genuine willingness on the part of partners to adapt to community priorities. The various studies suggest that partnership works best if it is embedded in pre-existing networks and relationships and a strong organising tradition at local level. But where this tradition exists, it has often been supported by local authority investment in a variety of activities, from small scale mutual support to community regeneration organisations (Thake, 1996). In Italy, Putnam (1993) has argued that local government is most effective in areas where there is a strong civil society. His concept of 'social capital' has attracted considerable interest in and beyond the UK. It is possible to argue, both in Italy and the UK, that there is a symbiotic relationship (Taylor and Bassi, 1996) and that good local government encourages the growth of civil society. A number of studies underline the importance of local government investment in community and voluntary organisations if there is to be a dynamic community input into partnership, but this investment is most likely to pay off if it allows for independent development.

Key themes and implications

History suggests that any system of welfare that depends too much on either government or the voluntary sector is doomed to failure. Some US commentators see a partnership between government and the voluntary sector as the best of all possible worlds, playing on the strengths of each sector to generate resources and produce responsive and yet equitable services (Salamon, 1989, pp. 10–11; Kramer, 1994). How far have current changes to local government gone to create this ideal?

There are two dominant formulations of the 'enabling' authority. In one formulation, the local authority is seen as the enabler of a market of welfare with a diversity of providers which offer choice to the consumer. Central government retains the power both over the purse strings and to define the rules of engagement. The alternative formulation is to emphasise the role of local government in 'enabling democracy', orchestrating the participation of a wide variety of interests in both the formulation and the implementation of policy. In this model, local government 'enables' a common framework through which diverse needs can be met in ways which meet social goals.

Whichever formulation is adopted there can be no doubt that we are on a steep learning curve. Sabatier (1993) argues that policy change needs to be studied over a decade or more to establish its impact. Much of the existing research on partnerships in service is still at the stage of conjecture or reporting on the special circumstances that have characterised initial stages of contracting in welfare. The experience and research on participation in policy has a longer pedigree, but suggests that there is still much to learn. More information is needed on the pressures and opportunities arising from changing funding patterns on different kinds of organisation, and current claims and fears need to be subjected to further scrutiny. However, it is important to recognise that these pressures and opportunities will be very different for a large national charity, an international campaigning body, a small self-help group and an umbrella body. They will also be different across policy fields and in different parts of the country.

The first implication that arises out of this review, therefore, is the need to continue to monitor the impact of changes both on the range of potential providers of welfare and on the users of changing services.

Subject to this, the themes arising from this review can be summarised under three main headings: market development; accountability; and sharing power.

Market and political development
Key themes
It is too early to say whether new systems of provision are likely to deliver a genuinely mixed economy of care either in terms of a wide variety of providers or of a range of different services for different levels of need. All the messages from the research reviewed here suggest that smaller and medium-sized organisations are at a considerable disadvantage in new markets and that even if they survive, they do so in conditions of insecurity and instability. The most favoured providers in new markets of welfare are likely to be the larger players,

or not-for-profits 'floated off' from statutory providers. Commercial markets – from newspapers to burgers – demonstrate the power of the large enterprise to dictate consumer preferences and choice. If welfare markets are to be different, government purchasing powers will need to be deployed in more imaginative ways.

In the community care field, researchers are calling for local authorities to become better informed about their local voluntary and community sector and to pick up the concepts of market and community development which were originally intended in the reforms. A 'pure market' does not exist in welfare (if indeed it does anywhere else). Industrial models of co-operation between purchasers and suppliers offer an alternative to the legalistic, arm's length purchasing models advanced by the more rigorous proponents of the market (Taylor and Hoggett, 1994). This requires that local authorities deploy a range of funding mechanisms and invest in the infrastructure that will enable smaller organisations and those providing 'complementary' services to benefit from new opportunities. This is especially important for excluded groups such as ethnic minority organisations. Otherwise the prediction is that large private or not-for-profit empires will eventually take over from the much maligned statutory service empires.

It is difficult to see how such a development role will be accommodated within the financial and performance constraints imposed by central government. There are currently significant disincentives to market development even in areas where the market needs to be stimulated, such as home care (Leat, 1993). Market development takes money away from much-needed services. Purchasers would anyway incur higher costs on a proliferation of smaller contracts. Money will continue to be tight, but radical changes in local government finance are needed if new resources are to be released in the voluntary and commercial sectors.

However, to focus only on market development is to ignore the interweaving of social and political with economic roles in the voluntary sector. In the 1980s, in defending itself against central government policies, local government took on a community and even political development role, being prepared to fund its critics and to put money into excluded communities to enable them to develop a voice in the political process (Wolch, 1990). This is a role that some continue but which is submerged in the culture of the market which finds little room for political accountability (Taylor, 1996). If pluralism and choice are not just to be confined to the powerful, if users and local communities are to develop the 'social capital' to invest in economic, social and environmental welfare and if public debate is to be enriched by a wide variety of views, then local authorities need to cast their development role wider than the market.

Finally, the experience of the 1980s suggests that voluntary and community organisations benefited from the tensions between central and local government and that, within reason, pluralism within government makes for pluralism within society. The move towards unitary authorities will change the picture once again and its impact on the voluntary and community sectors needs to be closely monitored.

Research issues

1. *Capacity and impact*

    What is the 'welfare mix' that is developing in different parts of the country between sectors? How are new market opportunities divided between different parts of the voluntary sector: national–local; large–small; national organisations, local organisations, new not-for-profits; user- and community-led organisations and those providing services for others? Who do purchasers go to when they need to develop new services?

    What is the turnover as contracts come up for renewal? Are they staying with the same providers? How 'secure' are they? What happens when contracts are renegotiated?

    Is there evidence of significant restructuring within the sector to meet new demands? What evidence is there of merger and rationalisation?

    How are individual voluntary and community organisations changing over time to meet new demands? What is the impact on the contribution and characteristics of volunteers and trustees?

    How are black and ethnic minority organisations affected by changing funding regimes, especially those whose needs and ways of working do not fit models developed in the traditional 'white' sector?

    How equipped are smaller voluntary organisations to take on mainstream services and what is the impact of their doing so? How does a move into service provision affect the advocacy and political roles of voluntary organisations?

How have the reforms affected users of mainstream services? Are 'complementary' services being lost and, if so, what is the impact on their current and potential users?

2.   *Support*
What models of purchasing offer most scope for diversity and development? Do decentralised models of government hinder or help the contribution of voluntary organisations both as service providers and as channels for participation in decision-making?

Where do voluntary organisations get their support from? What role is played by purchasers, intermediary bodies, national organisations and federations and franchising.

What support mechanisms do black and ethnic minority organisations use?

How are advocacy, development and 'non-essential' services being funded?

How is the role and funding of intermediary organisations changing with the reforms? Are they being forced into competition with their members?

What impact is local government reorganisation having on support (financial and in kind) for voluntary organisations of different kinds?

Accountability vs. autonomy
The potential replacement of public service empires with private service empires raises serious questions about accountability, which have already surfaced in relation to housing associations (Riseborough, 1995). The attenuation of the service chain is likely to complicate and confuse accountability. Although practice is variable across authorities (Deakin, 1996; Bemrose and MacKeith, 1996), there are dangers of 'institutional isomorphism' (DiMaggio and Powell, 1983), with new providers operating in the same way as the old.

Nonetheless, there are real tensions between regulation and safety on the one hand and flexibility and risk on the other, identified by nearly every researcher in this field. If markets in welfare are to supply flexibility and responsiveness to the consumer, new ways have to be found of reconciling these tensions.

Research issues

1. What forms of accountability are appropriate to new systems of welfare? What are the claims and expectations of funders, the public, users and other stakeholders? How are these being reconciled in different kinds of organisation? Who carries the can and what slips through the cracks?

2. Who has the power in contracts? How do power relationships develop over time? Is regulation getting tighter or looser? To what extent are powerful providers able to manipulate the purchaser and the public interest?

3. How can voluntary organisations and user- and community-based organisations be helped to develop their own standards and measures of quality? How do these compare with, and add to, purchaser-driven standards and measures?

4. What do leading-edge business models have to offer in developing a creative purchaser-provider relationship?

Sharing power

Voluntary organisations have an important role to play in producing not only 'willing, able and informed voters' (Wahlberg and Geddes, 1995) but active and informed participants between elections. However, the evidence on partnership is that, although some gains have been made, there is a very long way indeed to go before government can be said to 'belong to society' rather than the other way around. Other policy imperatives, financial constraints, staff resistance and insecurity all stand in the way of genuine community 'empowerment'. Much of the existing theory around policy networks suggests that voluntary and community organisations are unlikely to gain real influence except where they are already well-embedded in existing power structures. Partnership is not easy, but experience so far suggests that the commitment to such empowerment is still tenuous and that, despite pockets of good practice, more has been done to co-opt potential dissent than to share genuine power.

The incentives provided by central government have undoubtedly promoted partnership in areas that were resistant, but the centralisation of powers in UK governance is seen by some as a considerable and continuing hindrance to the involvement of voluntary and community organisations in local governance. Research also suggests that central government needs to develop its own links between separate departments and QUANGOs at the national level, and to be aware of the contradictions between some of its policies – particularly the effects of some of its funding policies on the development of small-scale activity (Taylor, 1995).

Locally, research so far suggests that partners need to develop a more sophisticated approach to questions of participative or representative democracy. Experimentation is needed to develop viable forms of community representation and to develop models for effective community and voluntary sector structures as a basis for partnership. Investment is needed in voluntary sector networks and infrastructure, which are vulnerable in the present funding climate but essential to effective community involvement.

Research issues

1. Why, after so many years, do communities still feel that the rhetoric of participation and partnership is not matched by reality? What are the persistent barriers to change and how can they be removed?

2. A number of new mechanisms for empowerment are emerging in the shape of citizens' juries, and so on. What role do community and voluntary organisations have in relation to these new ideas about empowerment?

3. The role of voluntary organisations in public life and debate has been under-researched (although see 6 and Randon, 1995). But many writers and researchers about the sector underline the significance of its advocacy role. How has this role developed over recent years and how is it affected by changed patterns of funding and delivery?

4. Are voluntary organisations still able to maintain a 'watchdog role' in a fragmented service environment where they have a vested interest as providers?

Comparative and multi-disciplinary research: a postscript

The process of carrying out the review raised two issues about the state of research in this field. The first is the separation that exists between the wider social and public policy research communities and the voluntary sector research community. The two discourses seem largely divorced from each other. Voluntary sector studies in this country could benefit hugely from more interaction with mainstream social and public policy traditions, their concepts, theories and debates, while social and public policy debates would be considerably enriched by more attention to the changing role of voluntary organisations as a 'gauge' of the shifting boundaries between public and private. More attention from the mainstream disciplines of sociology and political science would also enrich this debate. Even within voluntary sector studies, there is scope for more cross-fertilisation between policy areas. The issues facing environmental organisations, for example (see Young, 1994), or arts organisations, are conceptualised somewhat differently from those facing organisations in the social welfare field. There is a need for much greater cross-fertilisation.

Finally, this paper opened by contrasting the centralisation of government powers in the UK with decentralisation on the continent. In comparing European countries, Batley (1993, p. 225) contrasts two approaches: those which 'favour the marketisation of public services and the weakening of local government's role' and those which favour 'the reform of public services and the decentralisation of government so as to create the conditions for more diverse, flexible and responsive decision-making'. While the first was seen as essential to releasing the resources of voluntary and for-profit organisations by central government in the UK, the second has proved a fertile ground for the growth of the voluntary sector in parts of continental Europe.

The case for a democratically elected local government as a strong orchestrating force remains powerful (Stewart and Taylor, 1993; Stewart and Stoker, 1995; Roberts *et al.*, 1995). But Batley (1993) is far from arguing that local government in the UK should have been left alone. He argues that reforms in the UK, whatever the underlying ideology, have forced a much-needed change in local government from a preoccupation with service delivery to an enabling role more in keeping with the continental model. The practice of some local authorities in the UK, who have seen the promotion of a dynamic voluntary sector as part of good government, confirms that empowered local government and empowered voluntary and community organisations can go hand in hand – an argument that has been popularised by Putnam's work in Italy (1993). But old cultures die hard and this review suggests that there is still a long way to go before old patterns of patronage and control give way to a partnership that could play to the strengths of both sectors.

Notes

1. In this review, the term 'voluntary sector' is used to cover the voluntary and community sectors. 'Community sector' is used mainly when the review needs to emphasise the distinctive characteristics or needs of this part of the

sector. This review is concerned with what has been called the 'narrow' voluntary sector (6, 1991) – it does not include trade unions and public schools, political parties, universities and public schools.

2. The Commission on the Future of the Voluntary Sector (1996) cites Charity Commission evidence that 85 per cent of all full-time equivalent workers in charities are employed by just 8.6 per cent of charities.

3. The promotion of housing associations as the main provider of social housing is perhaps the clearest example of this.

4. Organisations in the broader voluntary sector, such as Rotary, Round Table, Freemasons, trade unions, political parties and some religious organisations are, of course, deeply embedded in decision-making structures and the effects of the changes on such bodies, though not part of this review, would make a fascinating study.

5. Lukes (1974) distinguishes between three faces of power: the power of A over B; the power to define the agenda within which A and B operate; and the power to define the way in which issues are institutionalised in society and hence how B internalises expectations and structures of power.

6. Leaders of tribes captured by the Aztecs were treated with unexpected ceremony – dressed up as princes and given everything they could desire for a year. But there was a catch. After this year, they were drugged and offered as a human sacrifice to the gods. Community representatives may feel some empathy with their situation!

References

Association of District Councils (1992) *Helping Communities Help Themselves: How District Councils Can Work with Voluntary Organisations.* London: Association of District Councils

Barnes, M., Harrison S., Wistow G. (1994) 'Consumerism and citizenship amongst users of health and social care services', paper presented to European Society for Medical Sociology Conference, Vienna, September

Batley, R. (1993) 'Comparisons and lessons', in R. Batley, and G. Stoker (eds) *Local Government in Europe: Trends and Developments.* London: Macmillan, pp. 210–29

Batley, R. and Stoker, G. (eds) *Local Government in Europe: Trends and Developments*. London: Macmillan

Bemrose., C and MacKeith, J. (1996) *Partnership for Progress: A Good Practice in the Relationship between Local Government and Voluntary Organisations*. Bristol: The Policy Press

Birchall, J., Pollitt, C. and Putnam, K. (1995) 'Freedom to manage? The experiences of NHS trusts, grant-maintained schools and voluntary transfers of public housing', paper presented at the UK Policy Studies Association Conference, York

Blackmore, M., Bradshaw, Y., Jenkinson, S., Johnson, N. and Kendall, I. (1995) 'The voluntary sector and quality assurance', paper presented to ESRC seminar: 'Challenges for Voluntary Agencies in a Changing Social Policy Environment', London: London School of Economics

Blackmore, M., Bradshaw, Y., Jenkinson, S., Johnson, N. and Kendall, I. (forthcoming) 'Intermediary organisations in the new welfare mix: a case study', accepted for publication in *Non-Profit Studies*

Blair, P. (1993) 'Trends in local autonomy and democracy: reflections for a European perspective', in R. Batley and G. Stoker (eds) *Local Government in Europe: Trends and Developments*. London: Macmillan

Brenton, M. (1985) *The Voluntary Sector in British Social Services*. London: Longman

Chanan, G. (1991) *Taken For Granted*. London: Community Development Foundation

Chanan, G. (1992) *Out of the Shadows*. European Foundation for Living and Working Conditions (also available form the Community Development Foundation)

Clapham, D., Kintrea, K. and Kay, H. (unpublished) 'The sustainability and maturity of community-based housing associations'

Clarke, G. (1995) *A Missed Opportunity: An Initial Assessment of the 1995 Single Regeneration Budget Approvals and their Impact on Voluntary and Community Organisations in England*. London: NCVO Publications

Clarke, J. (1995) 'The problem of the state after the welfare state', in M. May, E. Brunsdon and G. Craig (eds) *Social Policy Review 8*. London: Social Policy Association, pp. 13–39

Commission on the Future of the Voluntary Sector (1996) *Meeting the Challenge of Change: Voluntary Action into the 21st Century*. London: National Council for Voluntary Organisations

Craig, G. (1994) *The Community Care Reforms and Local Government Change*. Kingston-upon-Hull: University of Humberside

Deakin, N. (1995) ' The perils of partnership', in J. Davis Smith, R. Hedley and C. Rochester (eds) *An Introduction to the Voluntary Sector*. London: Routledge

Deakin, N. (1996) 'The devil's in the detail: contracting for social care by voluntary organisations', *Social Policy and Administration*, vol. 30, no. 1

Deakin, N. and Walsh, K. (1994) 'The enabling state: The role of markets and contracts', paper for Employment Research Unit Annual Conference, 'The Contract State? The Future of Public Management', Cardiff Business School, 27–8 September

DiMaggio, P. and Powell, W. (1983) 'The iron cage revisited: institutional isomorphism and collective rationality in organizational fields', *American Sociological Review*, vol. 48, pp. 147–60

Edwards, A. (1994) 'Local partnerships for crime prevention in England and Wales', *Urban Development Review*, July/August

Gibson, T. (1993) *Danger-Opportunity*. Telford: Neighbourhood Initiatives Foundation

Gidron, B., Kramer, R. and Salamon, L. (eds) (1992) *Government and the Third Sector: Emerging Relationships in Welfare States*. San Francisco: Jossey-Bass

Gutch, R. (1992) *Contracting: Lessons from the United States*. London: NCVO Publications

Hambleton, R., Essex, S., Mills, L. and Razzaque, K. (1995) *The Collaborative Council: A Study of Inter-agency Working in Practice*. Cardiff: Department of City and Regional Planning

Harris, H. (1996) 'He who pays the piper calls the tune: a consideration of management issues of voluntary and not-for-profit agencies in the contracting process', paper presented to the International Research Symposium on Public Services Management, Aston University, 25–26 March

Harris, M. (1993) 'Voluntary management committees: The impact of contracting', paper presented to 'Contracting: Selling or Shrinking', National Council for Voluntary Organisations and South Bank University, July 20–22

Hastings, A., McArthur, A. and McGregor, A. (1996) *Less than Equal? Community Organisations and Estate Regeneration Partnerships.* Bristol: The Policy Press

Houghton, P. and Timperley, N. (1992) *Charity Fundraising: A Guide to the Concept and Practice of Franchising Charitable Services.* London: Directory of Social Change

Hoyes, L., Jeffers, S., Lart, R., Means, R. and Taylor, M. (1993) *User Empowerment and the Reform of Community Care.* Bristol, SAUS Publications

Hunter, D. (1992) 'To market! To market! A new dawn for community care', *Health and Social Care*, vol. 1, pp. 3–10

Kendall, J. and Knapp, M. (1995) 'A loose and baggy monster', in J. Davis Smith, R. Hedley and C. Rochester (eds) *An Introduction to the Voluntary Sector.* London: Routledge

Kendall, J. and Knapp, M. (1996), *The Voluntary Sector in the UK.* Manchester: Manchester University Press

Kendall, J. and 6, P. (1994) 'Government and the Voluntary Sector in the United Kingdom', in J. Kendall and S. Saxon-Harrold (eds) *Researching the Voluntary Sector*, second edition. Tonbridge: Charities Aid Foundation

Knight, B. (1993) *Voluntary Action.* London: The Home Office

Kramer, R. (1994) 'Voluntary agencies and the contract culture: "dream or nightmare"', *Social Science Review*, March

Kramer, R., Lorentzen, H., Melief, W., Pasquinelli, S. (1993) *Privatization in Four European Countries: Comparative Studies in Government/ Third-sector Relationships.* Armonk, New York: M.E. Sharpe

Leat, D. (1988) *Voluntary Organisations and Accountability*. London: National Council for Voluntary Organisations

Leat, D. (1993) *The Development of Community Care by the Independent Sector*. London: Policy Studies Institute

Leat, D. (1995) ' Funding matters', in J. Davis Smith, R. Hedley and C. Rochester (eds) *An Introduction to the Voluntary Sector*. London: Routledge, pp. 157–89

Lewis, J. (1993) 'Developing the mixed economy of care: emerging issues for voluntary organisations', *Journal of Social Policy*, vol. 22, no. 2, pp. 173–92

Lewis, J. (1995) 'Welfare state or mixed economy of welfare', *History Today*, vol. 45, no. 2, pp. 4–6

Lewis, J., Bernstock, P. and Bowell, V. (1995) 'The community care changes: unresolved tensions in policy and issues in implementation', *Journal of Social Policy*, vol. 24, no. 1, pp. 73–94

Lewis, J. with Bernstock, P., Bovell, V., Wookey, F. (1996) 'The purchaser–provider split in community care: is it working?', *Social Policy and Administration*, vol. 30, no. 1, pp. 1–19

Lukes, S. (1974) *Power: a Radical View*. London: Macmillan

McCabe, A., Skelcher, C. and Nanton, P. (1994) *Networks in Urban Regeneration: A Report of Three Workshops Sponsored by the Joseph Rowntree Foundation*. Birmingham: Institute of Local Government Studies and Birmingham Settlement

MacFarlane, R. (1993) *Community Involvement in City Challenge*. London: NCVO Publications

Maloney, W.J., Jordan, G., and McLaughlin, A. (1994) 'Interest groups and public policy: the insider/outsider model revisited', *Journal of Public Policy*, vol. 14, no. 1, pp. 17–38

Martin, L., Gaster, L. and Taylor, M. (1995) *Client, Purchaser and Enabler Roles*. Luton: Local Government Management Board

Mercer, C. (1995) 'The big freeze', *Community Care*, 19–25 October

Mocroft, I. (1994) 'A survey of local authority payments to voluntary and charitable organisations, 1992/93', Charities Aid Foundation, *Dimensions of the Voluntary Sector*. Tonbridge: Charities Aid Foundation

NCVO News, May 1993

Nellis, M. (1995) 'Probation partnerships, voluntary action and community justice', *Social Policy and Administration*, vol. 29, no. 2, pp. 91–109

Newcastle Architecture Workshop (1990) *National Review of Architecture Workshops*. Newcastle: Newcastle Architecture Workshop

Norton, M. (1995) *Building on Innovation*. London: Directory of Social Change

Owen, D. (1964) *English Philanthropy: 1660–1960*. Cambridge: Harvard University Press

Page, D. (1994) *Developing Communities*. Sutton Hastoe Housing Association

Pinto, R. (1995) 'Revitalising communities: a moment of opportunity for local authorities', *Local Government Policy Making*, vol. 21, no. 5, May

Prins, M.C. (1995) 'Organisational change in small voluntary organisations: a study of twelve day centres and luncheon clubs for elderly people', paper presented to 'Researching the UK Voluntary Sector', National Council for Voluntary Organisations, 7–8 September

Putnam, R. (1993) *Making Democracy Work: Civic Traditions in Modern Italy*. Princeton, NJ: Princeton University Press

Reid, B.(1995) 'Interorganisational Networks and the Delivery of Local Housing Services', *Housing Studies*, vol. 10, no. 2, pp. 133–49

Reid, B. and Iqbal, B. 'Redefining housing practice: interorganisational relationships and local housing networks', in P. Malpass, (ed.) *The New Governance of Housing*. Longman, 1996

Richardson, J. (1995) *Purchase of Service Contracting*. London: National Council for Voluntary Organisations

Riseborough, M. (1995) 'Housing associations: voluntary, charity or non-profit bodies? An analysis of blurred boundaries', paper presented to conference on 'Researching the Voluntary Sector' at the National Council for Voluntary Organisations, September

Roberts, V., Russell, H., Harding, A., Parkinson, M. (1995) *Public/Private/ Voluntary Partnerships in Local Government*. Luton: Local Government Management Board

Russell, L., Scott, D. and Wilding, P. (1995) *Mixed Fortunes: the Funding of the Voluntary Sector*. Manchester: University of Manchester

Russell, L., Scott, D. and Wilding, P. (unpublished) 'The Funding of Local Voluntary Organisations'.

Sabatier, P.A. (1993) 'Policy change over a decade or more', in P.A. Sabatier and H.C. Jenkins-Smith (eds) *Policy Change and Learning: an Advocacy Coalition Approach*. Westview Press

Salamon, L.M. (1987) 'Partners in public service: the scope and theory of government–non-profit relations', in W.W. Powell (ed.) *The Nonprofit Sector: a Research Handbook*. New Haven: Yale University Press

Salamon, L.M. (1989) *Beyond Privatization: the Tools of Government Action*. Washington: The Urban Institute Press

Scott, R. and Meyer, J. (1993) 'The organization of societal sectors: propositions and early evidence' in W. Powell and P. DiMaggio (eds) *The New Institutionalism in Organizational Analysis*. Chicago: University of Chicago Press

Shore, P., Knapp, M., Kendall, J. and Carter, S. (1994) 'The local voluntary sector in Liverpool', in S. Saxon-Harrold and J. Kendall *Researching the Voluntary Sector*, second edition. Tonbridge: Charities Aid Foundation

6, P. (1991) *Defining the Voluntary and Nonprofit Sectors*. London: National Council for Voluntary Organisations

6, P. and Randon, A. (1995) *Liberty, Charity and Politics*. Aldershot: Dartmouth Publishing

Skelcher, C., McCabe, A., Lowndes, V. and Nanton, P. (1996) *Community Networks in Urban Regeneration*. Bristol: The Policy Press

Stewart, J. and Stoker, G. (eds) (1993) *Local Government in the 1990s*. London: Macmillan

Stewart, M. and Taylor, M. (1993) *Local Government Community Leadership*. Luton: Local Government Management Board

Stewart, M. and Taylor, M. (1996) *Empowerment and Estate Regeneration: A Critical Review*. Bristol: The Policy Press

Stoker, G. and Young, S. (1993) 'The contribution of third force organisations', in G. Stoker (ed.) *Cities in the 90s*. London: Longman

Taylor, M. (1995) *Unleashing the Potential: Bringing Residents to the Centre of Estate Regeneration*. York: Joseph Rowntree Foundation

Taylor, M. (1996) 'Between public and private: accountability in voluntary organisations', *Policy and Politics*, vol. 24, no. 1

Taylor, M. and Lansley, J. (1992) 'Ideology and welfare in the UK: the implications for the voluntary sector', *Voluntas*, vol. 3, no. 2, pp. 153–74

Taylor, M. and Lewis, J. (1993) 'Contracting: what does it do to voluntary and non-profit organisations', paper presented to 'Contracting: Selling or Shrinking', National Council for Voluntary Organisations and South Bank University, July 20–22

Taylor, M. and Hoggett, P. (1994) 'Trusting in networks/ the third sector and welfare change', in P. 6, and I. Vidal, (eds) *Delivering Welfare: Repositioning: Nonprofit and Co-operative Action in Western European Welfare States*. Barcelona: CIES

Taylor, M., Langan, J. and Hoggett, P. (1995) *Encouraging Diversity: Voluntary and Private Organisations in Community Care*. Aldershot: Arena

Taylor, M. and Bassi, A. (1996*)* 'Changing relationships between national and local government in two European countries: what are the implications for Third Sector Organisations in social care?', paper presented to the International

Society for Third Sector Research biennial conference: 'Citizen Participation, Economic Development and the Third Sector', Mexico City, July 1996

Taylor-Gooby, P. (1994) 'Charities in recession – hard times for the weakest?', in S. Saxon-Harrold, and J. Kendall (eds) *Researching the Voluntary Sector,* second edition. Tonbridge: Charities Aid Foundation

Thake, S. (1995) *Staying the Course: The Role and Structures of Community Regeneration Organisations.* JRF

Wahlberg, M. and Geddes, M. (1995) 'Taking the initiative on local democracy', *Local Government Policy Making,* vol. 21, no. 5, pp. 9–16

Wahlberg, M., Taylor, K. and Geddes, M. (1995) *Enhancing Local Democracy.* Luton: Local Government Management Board

Walsh, K. (1995) 'Working with contracts', Second ESRC Quasi-Markets Seminar, Bristol, School for Advanced Urban Studies

Ware, A. (1989) *Charities and Government.* Manchester University Press

Wistow, G., Knapp, M., Hardy, B. and Allen, C. (1992) 'From providing to enabling: local authorities and the mixed economy of social care', *Public Administration,* vol. 70, pp. 25–45

Wolch, J. (1990) *The Shadow State: Government and Voluntary Sector in Transition.* New York: The Foundation Center

Young, K. (1991) 'The future place of voluntary action: a discussion paper', paper presented to Gresham College seminar, Consumers Association, 19 April

Young S. (1995) 'Participation – out with the old, in with the new?' *Town and Country Planning,* April

Young, S. (1994) 'The contribution of non-profit organisations to sustainable development strategies in declining cities', paper prepared for the conference on 'The Politics of Sustainable Development: Theory, Policy and Practice within the European Union', October

4 Public attitudes to local government

Ken Young and Nirmala Rao

Every year, scores of national surveys of public attitudes to all manner of issues are undertaken by survey research companies. They range from opinion polls and limited inquiries into particular questions, made on behalf of clients with specific interests, to the vast multi-purpose annual British Social Attitudes survey (BSA). The reasons for undertaking these studies vary widely. Clearly, every commissioning client has in view a particular objective or interest, even if it is rarely as overt as in the case of pure market research. Local councillors have become nervously – and their officers perhaps more keenly – interested in commissioning studies of what their electors think. Not all surveys are so utilitarian. At the other end of the scale the academic appetite for knowledge for its own sake justifies such studies on the ground that anything knowable should be known.

This paper deals with attitudes to local government. In considering the condition of local government, the attitudes of many interested parties may be pertinent. Studies have been conducted into the attitudes of local authority employees, an exercise which at the national level produced few surprises.[1] (LGMB/MORI, 1994). More limited studies of MPs and civil servants have been undertaken,[2] as well as of councillors themselves,[3] and of members of appointed local boards.[4] But the major studies for our purpose are those of electors' (or public) attitudes.

This paper draws together the evidence presented by the five major comparable national studies of public attitudes to local government. We also draw on any other relevant source that appears to add to the cumulative total of our knowledge of attitudes to local government. The underlying purpose of the paper is two-fold. First, to assess what can be learned from this body of survey material. Secondly, to comment on the problems and limitations faced by studies of this sort in reflecting public attitudes.

Do public attitudes matter?

Do public attitudes matter? And, if so, why? That there *is* such a public interest in recording and interpreting public attitudes is the starting point of this paper. Although the importance to be accorded to local government itself is today a matter of dispute, few would contest that attachment to the institutions of democracy is of vital importance. Political attitudes, and their expression in citizen action (or inaction), provide the foundation for those institutions. Indifference, distrust or hostility may foreshadow their collapse. From this point of view, attitudes to local government are of intrinsic interest. Moreover, to explore them is to assert that the views of a narrow circle of 'people who matter' should not be the sole determinant of the shape our institutions take.

Acceptance that public attitudes matter is relatively recent. Under the terms of successive local government acts, local government arrangements are supposed to prove themselves 'effective and convenient'. The Commissioners appointed under the 1945 Local Government Act had been prepared to accept the view that 'the wishes of the inhabitants were most truly expressed by their elected representatives and their officials'. The guidelines laid down by the 1958 Act enjoined a wider process of direct consultation.[5] Under the 1972 Act, establishing what was convenient came to be recognised as requiring some test of the opinion of the electors themselves. The Local Government Boundary Commission for England, in the final stages of its life, commissioned a survey of attitudes to Humberside County Council. The present Local Government Commission has pushed this practice further still, commissioning a large programme of interviews with people affected by proposals for change.[6]

Public attitudes have also been monitored by local authorities in order to establish the extent to which people are satisfied with their performance.[7] In some cases, attitude surveys have been used as a form of propaganda or campaign material. The most notable example is the campaign mounted by the Greater London Council, which, when faced with the prospect of abolition, took its stand on the strong support accorded to it by ordinary Londoners.[8] Other local authorities have used attitude surveys ostensibly to monitor the success of their policies, although majority parties sometimes cannot resist turning any favourable results to their advantage as pre-election propaganda.

What is it that public attitude surveys measure? Leaving aside the possibility that results are affected by the survey method itself – and the major survey companies devote considerable effort to improving their methods in this regard – two sets of factors bear upon the responses. The first set of factors arise from the characteristics of the respondent him or herself, factors such as (for example) level of education, political involvement, or length of residence having a bearing on their views of local government and community politics. The second set of factors arise from living in a particular place and encountering its environment, its political life, and the public services provided there. Both shape, and are in turn shaped by, expectations of public services. Responses to local government surveys tend to be influenced, then, by an interaction between the two sets of factors, whose product might be termed *the subjective experience* of local government.

Most of the public attitude surveys undertaken have been locally commissioned, and tap that experience in a direct fashion.[9] The larger question of the national standing of local government itself – what might be termed 'the health of local government' issue – is also the subject of periodic surveys, usually by Royal Commissions and Committees of Inquiry. Thus, the Maud Committee on the Management of Local Government reported a comprehensive survey of the views of the local government elector that it carried out in 1965.[10] The Widdicombe Committee deliberately emulated this exercise twenty years later.[11] These two landmark surveys have since been complemented by three other national surveys: that conducted by the Joseph Rowntree Foundation's own research committee on local–central government relations, published in 1990;[12] the 1992 study by SCPR for the Department of the Environment;[13] and the 1994 British Social Attitudes survey, which included a module of local government questions, and which was similarly funded by the DoE.[14] These five studies are of particular importance for the depth and range of the evidence they offer. Others will be drawn on from time to time, including the 1984 BSA study, which included a small number of questions on local government.

The structure of this paper is as follows. In the next four sections we explore what people know of local government in general and how well they understand it. We ask how satisfied they are with their councils and councillors, and how ready they are to complain and protest against their decisions. We assess the strength of people's attachment to local democracy and ask what light survey evidence casts upon the habits of political participation. In each of these four broad themes, we look particularly for *trends* in public attitudes. In the final section, we attempt an overall assessment of what can be learned from the existing body of surveys and discuss some of the underlying problems that detract from their evidence on certain topics.

Awareness and knowledge

The working of local democracy is predicated upon the well-informed elector, knowledgeable about local affairs. Past surveys have been concerned with both awareness and knowledge of specific features of local government. Some studies have sought to assess the overall level of knowledge, classifying voters as more or less well-informed. In the light of these studies, how aware and knowledgeable *is* the local government elector?

Knowledge of local government services
Several of these surveys asked a series of questions inviting respondents to
identify which authority or other body was responsible for the provision of a list
of particular services. The services varied slightly between surveys, and have
included parks, libraries, schools, housing, hospitals, street cleaning and
lighting, electricity supply and unemployment benefit. Some of these services
were locally administered, some by county councils, and some by other public
bodies.

Table 4.1 Ability to correctly name provider of services

	1965 %	1985 %	1990 %	% change 1965 – 90
Street cleaning	83	80	77	-6
Refuse collection	98	79	83	- 15
Schools	87	67	70	-17
Housing	87	73	86	-1

Source: Maud, 1965; Widdicombe, 1985; JRF, 1990

Table 4.1 shows that levels of public knowledge of these matters is generally
high. Most respondents correctly identify the authority responsible for the
services they receive. Comparison with 1965 is slightly complicated; the Maud
Committee survey (Maud, 1965) asked people to identify spontaneously,
without prompting, any services which their local authority provided. Only at
the next stage were respondents offered a list of services and asked to identify
which authority provided them. So caution must be exercised, as it is difficult to
assess accurately the (probably negligible) question effect. That said, it would
appear that people in general had a rather better grasp of who was responsible
for the provision of local services in the 1960s than is the case today. There is no
immediately apparent explanation for this finding, although it may well be
explained by such factors as the delegation of education management functions
to schools, and the contracting out of street cleaning and refuse collection, as
well as a decreasing emphasis on civic education since the period when the
Maud survey was conducted.

Knowledge of local finance

Local accountability rests to a considerable extent on electors' responses to local expenditure decisions. But how thoroughly is the basis of local finance understood? A number of studies have explored knowledge of the local financial system, but none so thoroughly as the study carried out for the DoE in 1990 (DoE, 1992). The questions asked at that time covered the sources of money to pay for local services and their relative significance. They explored knowledge of the relative costs of council services, of the liability for rates (prior to the introduction of the community charge), and of responsibility for collecting and spending the rates, as well as of the factors which affect the rate levied.

Respondents for the DoE study showed in general a high level of knowledge of the sources of council money, with four out of five respondents correctly identifying the rates as a source of funding local services and over two-thirds mentioning central government grant in response to an unprompted question. With prompting, the majority of the remainder correctly identified the sources of finance, giving a total of 98 per cent aware of the rates, and 92 per cent aware of central government grant. About two-thirds identified the rates as the most important of the several sources of revenue, with 17 per cent thinking that most of the money spent was provided by central government.

Findings on the perceived cost of council services showed a reasonable grasp of the pattern of local expenditure. More than half identified education or housing as the most expensive service, with social services and police identified as the third and fourth most expensive.

When asked about the liability for rates, the majority of respondents correctly judged rates to be payable on all types of houses and flats, on offices and on industrial premises. Moreover, the grasp of the factors affecting the amount of rates payable was similarly good. Eighty-five per cent identified the size of the property as a determining factor, while just under half thought market values to be relevant. The best informed – just under a third – identified the level of rent that could be charged as a relevant factor, and a similar number cited such amenities as distance from shops and the possession of central heating. As few as one in ten imagined that the number of occupants determined the level of rates, and slightly fewer the occupants' income.

Overall, the educational level, status in the household, tenure, age, and sex of the respondent were associated with a grasp of local finance. Older and better-educated male heads of household were the most knowledgeable group in this survey.

Ability to name the council

The survey conducted for the Widdicombe Committee in 1985 asked respondents if they could name their local and county (in Scotland, regional) council. Seven out of ten respondents in Table 4.2 could name their local council, but only half could name their county or region. The JRF's follow-up study conducted five years later repeated these questions and recorded rather higher levels of correct response. The visibility and recognisability of particular local authorities obviously varies, and the differences recorded between different parts of Britain are quite striking. The low figure of awareness of the GLC – taken at the height of the campaign for its retention – is partly explained by the form of the question used by NOP.[15]

Table 4.2 Ability to correctly name local and county/regional council, by type of area (%)

	London	Met England	RoE&W	Scotland	Total
1985					
Local	81	65	73	52	70
County	38	45	57	52	52
1990					
Local	89	74	74	63	75
County	-	-	63	65	63
1992					
Local	92	73	77	-	69
County	-	-	73	-	73

Source: Widdicombe, 1985; JRF, 1990; DoE, 1992

Not surprisingly, those in the higher occupational groups and those whose education has been more extensive are more knowledgeable on this and on the other measures considered in this section. So too are men, and those who have lived in their locality for a longer period of time.

Ability to name the party in control of the local council

The second measure of political awareness used in those surveys was the ability to name the party in control of the local authority. In 1985, 61 per cent of all respondents correctly identified their controlling party at the local level, and rather less at the upper-tier level. Interestingly, there is rather less variation according to the personal characteristics of respondents, although men are commonly found to be more aware of local politics than women on this measure, and both surveys found a relationship between age and ability to name the party in control locally, although this was very much stronger in the second survey.

In comparison, where a person lives also has a considerable impact upon their awareness of local politics. Those in non-metropolitan England and in Wales, where, even in 1985, partisanship was more limited than elsewhere, were the least able to give a correct response. Scots were somewhat higher at 62 per cent, and Londoners higher still at 68 per cent. As many as 80 per cent of those living in metropolitan England could give a correct answer. Generally, then, party politics is both more vigorous and more clearly understood in the more urban areas. Awareness of political control is lower for county councils, with less than one in four able to correctly identify the controlling party in 1992, due in part no doubt to the prevalence of hung councils in these authorities after the 1989 elections, and the period of time which had elapsed since those elections took place.

Table 4.3 Awareness of party in control of the local council (%)

	1985	1992
Respondents able to correctly name party in control locally		
London	68	77
Metropolitan England	80	73
Non-metropolitan	53	61

Source: Widdicombe, 1985; DoE, 1992

The report of the 1990 survey presented some interesting findings on the extent to which awareness of the colour of the controlling party was shaped by the respondent's own politics. Whether Labour or Conservative supporters, respondents were far more likely to be able to identify their local controlling party if it was of the party which they themselves supported.

As Table 4.4 shows, this expression of political identification was stronger for Labour supporters than for Conservatives. At the same time, the tendency to be unaware of the controlling party circumstances where they did not share its party colour was also more marked for Labour than Conservative supporters.

Table 4.4 Awareness of party in control of the local council, by political sympathy (%)

	Con in Con area	Con in non-Con area	Labour in Lab area	Labour in non-Lab area
Correct	70	53	84	44
Incorrect	30	26	16	21
Not known	-	21	-	35

Source: JRF, 1990

Naming the local councillor

A third measure of awareness is the respondent's ability to name his or her local councillor. This ability does not vary by the respondent's gender (unlike many other measures), nor particularly by social class or housing tenure. It varied in 1985 very considerably according to type of area, age, and length of residence. Of particular note is the strikingly low level of recognition accorded to London councillors.

Table 4.5 Ability to correctly name local councillor (%)

Length of residence	
Up to 5 years	17
5 years or more	33
Region	
London	15
Met England	22
Rest of E&W	33
Scotland	42
Participation in elections	
Habitual voter	40
Occasional voter	22
Non-voter	14
All respondents	30

Source: Widdicombe, 1985

While there are no comparable national measures against which to assess the overall figure of 30 per cent, it is paralleled in local studies; in a study by MORI of Tower Hamlets in 1993 the overall figure was 32 per cent. Indeed, the finer-grained evidence of single-authority studies similarly suggests that inter-area variations predominate. In the Tower Hamlets study there was a strong association between overall levels of satisfaction with the council and ability to name a councillor. Equally, it appears from that and other local studies that councillors themselves vary in their visibility and recognisability, as some will play a prominent role in local affairs, and enjoy press publicity, while others will not. Questions of this sort may measure little of the real variation between respondents, but capture instead micro-level variations in the nature of local politics.

A measure of general knowledge

The 1985 Widdicombe study, the 1990 JRF study and that conducted by SCPR for the DoE in 1992 all attempted to assess the overall level of respondents' *general* knowledge of local government by scoring their answers to the whole range of questions discussed here. In all three cases scales were created: the Widdicombe and DoE studies used similar but not identical four-point scales, ranging from 'well', 'quite well', 'not very well' informed to 'uninformed'. The JRF study used two categories of 'relatively well-informed' and 'ill-informed'. Although there were some slight variations in question content, the number of items was the same in each case, and the break points similarly defined. Table 4.6 was constructed to enable comparison across the three surveys by collapsing the Widdicombe and SCPR categories and relabelling them to correspond with those of the JRF study. The findings are remarkably similar, suggesting that this is a robust method of assessing overall knowledge.[16]

Table 4.6 Overall knowledge of local government (%)

	1985	1990	1992
Well-informed	52	53	57
Ill-informed	48	47	43

Source: Widdicombe, 1985; JRF, 1990; DoE, 1992

Table 4.7 gives both the summary figures for 1985 (Widdicombe) and 1990 (JRF) together with the overall breakdown by age group, and again shows a striking consistency across both surveys. The 1992 (DoE) study, in its published form, used different age categories, making direct comparison impossible without recourse to the original data. Nevertheless, the overall pattern is similar, with the oldest and youngest groups being less knowledgeable than the middle-aged. All of these studies show that the better educated, and those in professional or managerial jobs are far more knowledgeable than others.

Table 4.7 Overall knowledge of local government by age group

	18–34 %	35–54 %	55–64 %	65 + %	all %	(base)
Respondent is well-informed about local government						
1985	47	56	60	46	52	1,144
1990	50	61	64	49	53	1,164

Source: Widdiciombe, 1985; JRF, 1990

Satisfaction with local authorities

There has been a growing interest in surveys of the extent to which people are satisfied with their local authorities. The new requirements on Charter indicators to which local authorities have been subjected by the Audit Commission have given further impetus to this development. And, while we argue in the concluding section of this paper that the use of local satisfaction measures is sometimes fraught with difficulty, there is still some profit in comparing the overall results of successive national surveys in order to establish whether or not changes have occurred over time. It is possible to compare findings for different years in respect of the general levels of satisfaction with councils, with councillors, and with specific services. There is also useful material concerning complaints against councils and on people's willingness to protest against unpopular decisions.

Overall satisfaction with the local council

Since the 1980s, a number of surveys have sought to measure overall satisfaction with local councils. Among these is the series undertaken on behalf of the National Consumer Council (NCC), whose 1991 and 1995 surveys provide a measure of change during a period when local authorities have been devoting increasing efforts to satisfying their public.[17] Responses to the question *'how strongly do you agree or disagree that quality of local council services is good overall?'* showed an overall increase in agreement of ten percentage points – from 51 to 61 per cent – over the four-year period, this change being fairly consistent across all sub-groups.

Table 4.8 Overall satisfaction with local council, by 'political sympathy' (%)

	1985	1990
Agree local council		
runs things 'very' or 'fairly' well		
Conservatives in Conservative area	72	86
Conservatives in non-Conservative area	63	75
Labour in Labour area	65	78
Labour in non-Labour area	70	73
Politically sympathetic to local council	68	82
Politically unsympathetic to local council	66	76

Source: Widdicombe, 1985; JRF, 1990

A different question form has been used in other surveys, focusing on the extent to which respondents judge their local council to 'run things well'. Yet it is not always clear just what is being measured by questions of this sort. As with the nationally equivalent questions, responses are coloured by partisan judgements: people are more satisfied with governments of their own political colour, and less so with those whom they do not support. The Widdicombe (1985) and JRF (1990) surveys showed that people living in areas where the political control of the council corresponds with their own preferences tend to be more satisfied, this being especially true of Conservatives, who discriminate in this way more sharply than do Labour supporters. The 1985 study threw up one exception, showing Labour voters in Labour areas to be the most dissatisfied; this finding was not reproduced five years later and, as Table 4.8 shows, there appears to be a modest general association between political sympathy and approval of the council.

Rather more meaningful are questions about satisfaction with particular services, into which a number of national surveys have enquired. Again, the 1995 NCC study is the most recent of those available. Table 4.9 shows the pattern of change between 1991 and 1995 in a range of specific services. Comparison with an earlier survey undertaken on behalf of the NCC in 1986 gives a picture of fluctuating responses in respect of some services, with 1995 levels returning broadly to 1986 levels after a marked dip. This broad picture should be borne in mind when interpreting the NCC's earlier general satisfaction figures.[18]

Table 4.9 Satisfaction with specific council services, 1986, 1991 and 1995 (%)

	Very/fairly satisfied		
	1986	1991	1995
Environmental			
Refuse collection	85	81	91
Street lighting	80	77	81
Footpaths/street cleaning	44	41	53
Road maintenance	29	30	43
Leisure			
Libraries	78	68	70
Swimming pools and sports facilities	61	55	55
Parks, playgrounds and open spaces	63	55	54
Education			
Primary schools			
All	43	43	54
Child 5–10 yrs in household	76	70	81
Secondary schools			
All	34	37	46
Child 11–14 in household	60	60	78

Source: NCC, 1995

Of particular note in this table is the effect that *service use* has on *service satisfaction:* only 43 per cent of all respondents were satisfied with primary schools in 1991 (54 per cent in 1995); when those without a primary school-aged child in the household are filtered out, however, this figure rises to 70 per cent (81 per cent in 1995), indicating that satisfaction measures may give meaningless results without such filters.

A more general and cautionary point follows from this difference in the responses of users and non-users. People who are differently placed within society may view a similar public service in very different terms, and are responding to what they subjectively experience as a different question. Thus, owner-occupiers generally return much more negative responses about council houses than do council tenants themselves. But while tenants are passing judgement about the experience of living in these properties, owner–occupiers are seemingly responding to the external architectural and social impact of council estates, or to stereotypes of the people who live there. Examples of this sort could be readily multiplied.

Satisfaction with councillors

It is unusual in democratic societies for people to express particularly high
levels of satisfaction with their elected representatives. Indeed, levels of
satisfaction with councillors in Britain tend to be quite low; those with MPs
lower still. Miller's ESRC study, still in progress at the time of writing, similarly
suggested that 92 per cent agree that 'Parliament and Government waste
resources', while only 57 per cent believe local councils do so. General measures
of satisfaction at this level are fairly meaningless. As with much attitudinal
research, the real value lies not in the aggregate measurement but in the ability
to compare and contrast sub-groups in the population.

The 1994 BSA study deployed a considerable number of rather more specific
questions about attitudes to councillors. At the most general level, it sought
responses to two statements:

Generally speaking those we elect as councillors lose touch with people pretty quickly.

Councillors don't care much what people like me think.

Table 4.10 summarises the overall response.

Table 4.10 Attitudes towards councillors (%)

	Agree/ agree strongly	Neither agree nor disagree	Disagree/ disagree strongly
Councillors ...			
Lose touch with people pretty quickly	47	28	23
Don't care much what people like me think	36	28	34

Source: British Social Attitudes, 1994

Although nearly half of the respondents agreed that councillors 'lose touch
pretty quickly', comparison with attitudes to MPs suggest that satisfaction with
councillors is at a comparatively high level. Moreover, negative views of
councillors are associated with both educational level and claimed interest in
politics, the better-educated and more interested electors being less likely to
dismiss the councillor as out of touch and uncaring. The differences are sufficient

to suggest a degree of alienation from the political system on the part of that very large minority of the population who have no educational qualifications.

Table 4.11 Attitudes towards councillors, by education and political interest (%)

	Agree councillors...	
	lose touch	don't care
Education		
Degree	23	15
No qualifications	50	48
Interest in politics		
High	39	29
Moderate	49	35
Low	56	41

Source: British Social Attitudes, 1994

While Miller's study focused on councils rather than councillors, a similarly worded question produced 39 per cent agreement that 'councils don't care' about the respondent's opinions, and somewhat higher figures for TECs and health authorities. Differences on another measure, perceptions of whether these institutions had 'the good of the community at heart' produced small differences, while Miller's respondents appear not to distinguish between the members of local authorities and appointed bodies in respect of their likelihood of being motivated by a 'sense of duty'.

Complaining

Attitude questions of this sort pose generalities which may not reflect actual experience. The Widdicombe (1985) survey asked those respondents who had contacted or complained to their council how satisfied they were with the outcome. Those who had contacted councillors were somewhat more satisfied with the way the matter was dealt with than those who had been dealt with by officers. This higher level of satisfaction with councillors was much more marked in cases where the respondent had actually gone so far as to lodge a complaint. The study undertaken by SCPR for the DoE in 1992 similarly explored these issues, and the Table 4.12 shows some closely comparable results with regard to the satisfaction about the outcome of the complaint. Councillors clearly give much greater satisfaction to the complaining resident than do officers. It is possible that this gap may close up over time (or indeed may already have done so), as the norms of public service management increasingly come to reflect the 'customer care' ethos derived from private sector management.

Table 4.12 Satisfaction with outcome of contact or complaint (%)

| | Very or fairly satisfied | |
	1985	1992
Complained to councillor	43	43
Complained to officers	26	30

Source: Widdicombe, 1985; DoE, 1992

The 1992 DoE study replicated the Widdicombe question form with respect to complaints, providing a basis for ready comparison, except in respect of the actual subject matter of complaints, where different categories were offered in the two studies. Who complains the most? The middle aged were found to be the most likely to want to complain in both surveys; otherwise, the differences between social groups are not great. Both surveys also probed respondents' reasons for not complaining – as did the 1995 NCC study – and with similar results.

As Table 4.13 shows, the figures correspond closely, suggesting that this is indeed a useful and reliable measure. Table 4.14, taken from the 1992 study, shows a strong age effect, and a less strong class effect, on some of the most commonly cited reasons for not complaining.

Table 4.13 Reasons for not complaining (%)

	1985	1992
There was no point	29	31
No time	17	23
Somebody else complained	10	12
Did not know how to complain	8	11
Laziness	14	8
Problem resolved itself	3	4
Didn't feel so strongly	3	4
Somebody else should have complained	4	2
Other reason	13	16
Don't know	4	1

Source: Widdicombe, 1985; DoE, 1992

The 1995 National Consumer Council study looked in more detail at complaints by consumers, finding that nearly eight in ten consumers would complain if they were dissatisfied with council services, while 22 per cent would not complain at all, even if they were dissatisfied. Comparison with an earlier study in 1980 by the same body suggests that a continuing minority of respondents gave up on complaining because they had no confidence in its likely impact. Complaints are but one way of registering dissatisfaction, however. In more extreme cases, the individual may be moved to go beyond complaining to directly challenge local decisions.

Table 4.14 Reasons for not complaining, by age and socio-economic status (%)

	No point	No time	Did not know how to
Age			
18–24	25	25	21
25–44	29	27	11
45–59	35	23	11
60 or over	37	14	5
Socio-economic group			
Professional/managerial	38	19	9
Other non-manual	26	28	11
Skilled manual	34	22	10
Semi-skilled manual	27	19	20
Unskilled	30	21	9

Source: DoE, 1992

Challenging local decisions

In the classic 1960 study of the *Civic Culture*, Almond and Verba asked a question about what actions a respondent would take if faced with an unjust or harmful action by the legislature or, separately, by their local council.[19] The responses to that question have formed the basis for subsequent enquiries into active citizenship, focusing on the propensity to act, on the channels chosen for protesting, and on beliefs as to their relative efficacy.[20]

The standard question has been used on a number of occasions in the BSA series, although only rarely in relation to local action, and in the JRF (1990) study. A more elaborated version has been used, with some changes, in the Widdicombe (1985) and DoE (1992) studies, but the differences in the categories offered were too great to be worth exploring here. Tables 15 and 16 (overleaf) show the changes over time between the 1984 and 1990 surveys, with respect to the actions people *would take*, and those they *expect to be most effective*.

Table 4.15 Responses to the prospect of an unjust or harmful action (%)

	1984	1990
Personal action		
Contact councillor	61	65
Speak to influential person	14	19
Contact council official	26	27
Contact media	18	27
Collective action		
Sign petition	50	49
Raise issue in an organisation	6	11
Go on a protest or demonstration	8	12
Form a group of like-minded people	10	12
None of these	5	5

Source: British Social Attitudes, 1984; JRF, 1990

Table 4.16 Most likely effective response to an unjust or harmful action (%)

	1984	1990
Personal action		
Contact councillor	38	33
Speak to influential person	5	6
Contact council official	8	5
Contact media	16	18
Collective action		
Sign petition	14	12
Raise issue in an organisation	2	2
Go on a protest or demonstration	4	5
Form a group of like-minded people	5	3
None of these	5	6

Source: British Social Attitudes, 1984; JRF, 1990

This simpler form of table lends itself to an even more compressed expression in a single index for both individual and collective action. This has proved a particularly useful measure for discriminating between groups in the population in terms of their propensity to protest or take action against their local council.

The two indexes – the Personal Action Index (PAI) and Collective Action Index (CAI) are calculated by simple formulae thus:

$$\frac{P \text{-} i}{n} \quad \text{or} \quad \frac{C \text{-} i}{n}$$

where P is the number of personal actions mentioned, C the number of collective actions, i the number or people choosing none of the proffered courses of action and n the number of respondents in that sub-group of the sample. Possible scores on either range from -1 (no respondent chooses any of the possible course of action) to +4 (every respondent chooses all four courses of action, no abstainers). PAI and CAI scores vary over a narrower range in practice, high scores on the first being closely associated with higher education and social class, middle age and male gender, while CAI scores, while broadly similar, are additionally driven by such factors as trade union membership. CAI scores may also be more volatile both nationally and locally than PAI.

With more instances of the question being asked in its Parliamentary than its local council form, there is a better time series for national than for local protest. Comparison of results at both levels reveals that the propensity to protest local government actions is higher than that recorded for Parliamentary actions, reflecting the greater closeness of local government to the aggrieved citizen. Both show a tendency to increase over time. Table 4.17 shows the scores drawn from the 1984 BSA survey, and calculated from that conducted for the JRF in 1990.

Table 4.17 Protesting local council actions, 1984 and 1990

	1984	1990
PAI	1.13	1.32
CAI	0.69	0.79

Source: British Social Attitudes, 1984; JRF, 1990

Additionally, the political action question has also been used in local level surveys undertaken by MORI, enabling fruitful comparisons to be made between national scores and those achieved in particular local authority areas, as well as between those areas. Sub-group differences are of particular interest, and the 1994 MORI study of Tower Hamlets was so designed as to permit fine-grained analysis by neighbourhood, and by ethnic group.[21] In both respects, PAI and CAI scores varied markedly, and Table 4.18, which shows the extent of variations between different ethnic groups, highlights the unusually low collective action scores recorded by the borough's largely Bangladeshi Asian population.

Table 4.18 Protesting local council actions in Tower Hamlets, 1994

	PAI	CAI
White	1.24	0.96
Asian	0.99	0.38
Afro-Caribbean	1.04	0.63

Source: MORI, 1993

Attachment to local government

We turn now to the most basic and enduring of all the issues in relation to the public's attitudes to local government: that of its attachment to local government as an institution. Two common measures are of particular interest: attitudes to local autonomy and to its antithesis, central government control; and attitudes to the locally representative character of local government.

Central control of local government

One of the most effective measures of the strength of people's attachment to local government is their belief that councils should not be more controlled by central government than they are at present. Since 1983 the BSA series has asked:

> *do you think that local councils ought to be controlled by central government more, less or about the same amount as now?*

There has not been a very marked change in the pattern of opinion on this issue over the 11-year period, although there are some signs of a watershed in 1987, the first year of Mrs Thatcher's third term, when the public impact of her proposed measures is likely to have been sharply increased. The average level of support for central control *after* that year rose by about three percentage points (see Table 4.19), as did support for increased local autonomy, suggesting that there has been a greater acceptance of the realities of central control since that time.

Not surprisingly, after 15 years of Conservative government this is an issue on which respondents divide according to their party predilections. Although almost half of Labour and Liberal Democrat supporters wish to see less control by central government, seven in ten Conservatives are either content with the status quo or would be happy to see more central control (see Table 4.20).

Table 4.19 Trends in attitudes towards central control (%)

	1983	1984	1985	1986	1987	1989	1990	1994
Local councils should be controlled by central government								
More	13	14	14	15	19	16	20	16
About the same	45	42	46	36	34	37	34	40
Less	34	36	33	37	37	38	35	39

Source: 1985 Widdicombe, all other years BSA

Table 4.20 Attitudes to central control, by party identification (%)

	Con	Labour	Lib Dem
Local councils should be controlled by central government			
More	23	12	11
About the same	46	36	39
Less	28	48	46

Source: British Social Attitudes, 1994

Earlier surveys asking the same question in 1985 (Widdicombe) and 1990 (JRF) showed particularly strong support for increased central control among Conservatives living in non-Conservative areas. But responses to rather general questions about the desired level of 'central control' should, however, be treated with caution. A far better measure is obtained on the more specific and tangible issue of whether the level of local taxation should be entirely a matter for local authority to decide or whether central government should have the final say. BSA figures showed a fairly consistent large majority supporting local determination of rate levels from 1984 onward, although the imminent introduction of the poll tax in 1990 caused a noticeable movement in favour of central government.

The latest figures in 1994 are the first since the introduction of council tax, and Table 4.21 compares these with the 1984 figures. Some caution is probably called for in interpreting these figures, as the absence of a fixed wording for this question (shifting from 'rates' to – in the intermediate years – 'poll tax' and then to 'council tax') may have coloured responses especially among the less well-informed electors. Nevertheless, the shifts which have occurred over a ten-year period have been in favour of more central control, and are to be found in all three parties. The key figure is the percentage point change in favour of central determination of local taxation: 13 points in the case of Conservatives, 14 for Liberal Democrats, and 10 in the case of Labour supporters.

Table 4.21 Who should decide local taxation, by party identification, and change 1984–1994

	Conservative		Labour		Liberal Democrat	
	1994 %	change 1984–94	1994 %	change 1984–94	1994 %	change 1984–94
Local councils	55	-10	74	-10	69	-11
Central gov't	42	+13	21	+10	28	+14
Don't know	3	- 3	5	-	4	2

Source: British Social Attitudes, 1984 and 1994

Expectations of councillors

Attachment to the idea of local government involves more than a simple preference for the local determination of service and taxation levels. Equally important is the belief that the councillor as the elected representative is the cornerstone of local democracy. But what are councillors for? And how should they approach the task of representation? Should they be concerned primarily to take up complaints or manage the council services?

The 1994 BSA survey asked a number of relevant questions, covering the most important activities for councillors, what they should pay regard to when deciding on issues of local importance, and the extent to which they are trusted to behave as properly accountable representatives. On the first of these, respondents were asked:

> *which of the following do you think is the more important for a councillor to do: to take up problems and complaints people have about the council's services; or to help manage the council's services so that they are run as well as possible?*

Overall, there is a stronger preference for councillor involvement in the management of services, and this is considerably stronger for more highly educated respondents, and for owner-occupiers (Table 4.22).

Perhaps the sharpest measure of the representative expectation is the extent to which electors expect their councillors to give priority to their local interests rather than their own personal views or those of their party. The 1994 BSA survey sought this information and also made the customary distinction between ward interests and those of the whole local authority area. Table 4.23

shows the remarkable extent of agreement that councillors should follow neither their own views nor those of their party. It also shows the rather more variable division between the local ward and the interests of the wider local authority area as claims on the councillor's attention.

Table 4.22 Most important activities for councillors (%)

	To take up problems	To manage services
Education		
Higher education	32	56
'A' or '0' level	38	52
CSE or none	46	44
Tenure		
Owner-occupier	37	52
Local authority tenant	46	42
Other renting	43	43
All respondents	40	50

Source: British Social Attitudes, 1994

Table 4.23 Expectations of councillors' actions on local issues, by age, education and tenure (%)

	Councillors should consider...				
	own views	ward interests	whole area	party's views	can't choose
Age					
18–24	2	18	74	2	5
25–44	1	42	50	2	5
45–64	1	44	50	1	2
65+	2	42	50	1	5
Education					
Degree	1	46	49	1	2
No qualifications	2	35	54	2	6
Tenure					
Owner-occupier	1	43	52	2	3
Council tenant	3	37	51	2	7
Other rented	1	35	56	1	5
All respondents	1	40	52	2	5

Source: British Social Attitudes, 1994

Table 4.24 Trust in councillors to put the interests of the area above party (%)

	Always/ most of time	Some of the time	None of the time
Party identification			
Conservative	36	49	13
Labour	29	53	14
Liberal Democrat	37	54	9
Other/none/DK	21	47	21
Age group			
25–44	31	53	13
45–64	32	50	16
65 and over	31	47	17

Source: British Social Attitudes, 1994

Finally, if people would prefer to see councillors act in deference to local interests, it does not follow that they *trust* their councillors actually to do so, particularly where their party allegiance is involved. Table 4.24 shows a rather sceptical response, with some difference in levels of trust.

Participation

However well or poorly-supported local self-government may be in terms of attitudes to central control and confidence in councillors, its actual standing in practice rests upon the willingness of people to participate in the electoral process. There are of course degrees of participation, which may take the limited form of voting, of playing a more direct part in local affairs by attending local council meetings, or of actually standing for election.[22]

Voting

The classic expression of public attitudes to a particular local authority is the casting – or withholding – of a vote by electors. Elections are episodic, and ambiguous in their interpretation. Attitude and opinion surveys have become a popular means of filling that interpretative gap. Three points about British local voting behaviour have attracted the most comment. The first is the relatively low electoral turnout in Britain, compared with other European countries, (though not, notably, with the USA); it has also been argued that electoral turnout in Britain has been in long-term decline. Table 4.25 shows some comparative figures.[23]

Table 4.25 Local election turnout: comparative figures (%)

	Range	Mean
Sweden	80–98	90
Denmark	75–85	80
Italy	80–90	85
France	65–75	70
New Zealand	40–67	53
Britain	20–60	40
Australia	30–40	35
Canada	25–40	33
USA	15–40	25

Source: Goldsmith, 1992

However, while the number who cast a vote is clearly recorded, virtually all surveys of reported voting behaviour in the United Kingdom overstate the actual vote. The 1994 BSA study was no exception, with an overall figure of 59 per cent of those eligible to vote, and having the opportunity to do so in 1993 or 1994, claiming to have voted (Table 4.26). This familiar overstatement is often taken as casting doubt on the validity of self-reported voting as a measure, but (selective memory and confusion aside) three factors go some way to explain the discrepancy.

Table 4.26 Voting in district council elections (%)

	Claimed to have voted in last local election
Age	
18–24	34
25–44	59
45–59	67
60 and over	75
Tenure	
Owner-occupier	65
Council tenants	58
Private renters	49
All respondents	59

Source: British Social Attitudes, 1994

The first is non-response bias: people who refuse to take part in a survey of this type are more likely to have abstained from voting at the last election. The second is response bias: people are more likely to claim that they have voted whether they did or not. This is in part a reflection of social norms, which encourage over-reporting on such a sensitive issue. It may also be the case that there is a tendency for those who agree to be interviewed to be more inclined than refusers to conform to those pressures and expectations. The third factor is not concerned with reporting of voting behaviour, but with the actual turnout rates with which they are compared. Electoral registers contain an element of deadwood, including people who occupy two homes, those who have moved but have not been deleted from their old address, and those who have died since the register was compiled. The best available estimate suggests that these three factors each account for about a third of the discrepancy between 'actual' and reported voting.[24]

Table 4.27 Voting in district council elections, by attitudinal characteristics (%)

	Claim to have voted in last election
Interest in local politics	
Great deal/fair amount	83
Not much	62
None at all	38
Community involvement	
Active in local organisation	80
Not-active	59
Length of residence in local area	
Up to 1 year	23
1–5 years	39
6–10 years	48
10 years and over	54

Source: DoE, 1992

So what factors might induce people to turn out to vote? No simple explanation is available, as a range of factors seem to bear upon that decision. The first group of factors are specific to the political circumstances of the locality, and include the degree of political competition or marginality of control of the council, and the intensity of party campaigning. This itself may reflect the type of area: one-class (or one-party) areas tend to have a lower turnout. The second group of factors relate to the characteristics of the individual elector, both demographic and attitudinal. Age, education and social class all have a bearing on the propensity to vote at local elections. While there are no differences between men and women, older electors are more likely to vote than are younger people.

Reported voting is also associated with knowledge about, and interest in, politics. Likewise, so too is the respondent's attitudes to party politics, their level of knowledge and awareness of local affairs, and their involvement in them. Voting in local elections is also associated with involvement in local organisations. Four out of five of those who are active members of local bodies claimed to have voted in the last district elections, compared with 59 per cent of those who are not active. Similarly, those who have lived longer in the locality are more likely to vote than are younger and more transient people.

The low turnout typical of British local elections suggests a lack of commitment to, or belief in, the process of local representative democracy. This might be due to three factors. The first is the belief that local elections make no difference, either because local councils are not the arbiters of what happens locally, or because the actions of the competing parties are too similar to offer a real choice to the elector. Lack of commitment may also be due to the incomprehensibility of the electoral process itself. The 1994 BSA survey explored these matters in a series of questions aimed to elicit agreement or disagreement with a series of statements.

Table 4.28 (overleaf) shows that scarcely more than half the respondents believe that local election results determine how matters are run locally. Despite this, only a quarter of the respondents agree with the statement that there is no point in voting 'because it makes no difference who gets in', while less than a third find local elections 'too complicated'.[28]

Since the Maud Committee enquiry of 1965, similar questions have been used from time to time although, regrettably, different studies have not used common questions consistently. However, a comparison limited to these two measures is possible. Table 4.29 (overleaf) shows that there has been a steep and continuing decline in people's belief that local elections decide how things are run locally. These findings have been explored in the authors' contribution to the 1995 BSA volume.

Table 4.28 Attitudes to the electoral process (%)

	Agree strongly/ agree	Neither	Disagree/ disagree strongly
The way people decide to vote in local elections is the main thing that decides how things are run in this area	54	26	17
There is no point in voting in local elections because in the end it makes no difference who gets in	26	18	54
Local elections are sometimes so complicated that I really don't know who to vote for	30	20	48

Source: British Social Attitudes, 1994

Table 4.29 Attitudes to the local electoral process: 1965–1994 (%)

	1965	1985	1994
The way that people vote in local elections is the main thing that decides how things are run in this area	77	60	54
Local council elections are sometimes so complicated that I really don't know who to vote for	29	34	30

Source: Maud, 1965; Widdicombe, 1985; British Social Attitudes, 1994

Party politics in local government

Although party politics are by no means a new feature of local government, the period since reorganisation in 1974 has seen a further spread of partisan competition to areas where councils were hitherto run on ostensibly non-party lines. How have people in general responded to these developments?

First, attitudes to the presence of party politics in local government. The 1965 Maud Committee survey indicated that for a large proportion of the electorate, party politics were seen as an unwelcome intrusion. At that time, it was the most commonly cited criticism of the working of the democratic process in local government.[26] The 1985 Widdicombe survey and the 1994 BSA asked an identically worded question:

> *In most areas all councillors come from one of the political parties and councils are organised on party lines. There are some areas where most councillors are independent and the council is not organised on party lines. Which do you personally think is the better system ... the party system or the non-party system?*

Differences in the wording of the *responses* to the question – the 1994 BSA study offered an additional choice of 'can't choose' – underlie the differences in Table 4.30. Particularly striking, however, is the stability of the minority of one third of respondents who opt for the party system in both years shown in Table 4.30.[27]

Table 4.30 Attitudes to the party system in local government (%)

	1985	1994
Councils are better run with ...		
The party system	34	34
The non-party system	52	33
Don't know/can't choose	14	33

Source: Widdicombe, 1985; British Social Attitudes, 1994

Table 4.31 (overleaf) shows there to be a quite marked correspondence between support for the party system and the extent of its prevalence in the respondent's home area. The grip of party politics is weaker in the more rural areas, and this is reflected to a degree in the responses of people living in different types of area[28]. There is also a strong relationship between attitudes to party politics and support for different political parties. While only a minority prefer the party system, the 1994 BSA study showed a widespread acceptance of it at election time. More than half of the respondents claim to vote for their preferred party, regardless of the candidate. A further 28 per cent vote for the party on the condition that they approve of the candidate, while only a small minority would vote for the candidate irrespective of their party affiliation (Table 4.32). And, as Table 4.33 (overleaf) shows, it is Labour supporters who most strongly favour party, while Liberal Democrats' support is the most conditional, a considerable proportion of them preferring to make a judgement about the candidate.

Table 4.31 Attitudes to party politics in local government (%)

	Party system	Non-party system	DK/can't choose
Density			
Most rural	30	40	30
Rural	30	36	33
Urban	38	30	32
Most urban	38	25	36
Party identification			
Conservative	35	39	26
Labour	43	26	31
Liberal Democrat	25	43	32

Source: British Social Attitudes, 1994

Table 4.32 Voting for party or candidate (%)

Respondent ...	
Votes for party, regardless of candidate	52
Votes for party, only if approves of candidate	28
Votes for candidate, regardless of party	6
Doesn't vote	14

Source: British Social Attitudes, 1994

Table 4.33 Voting for party or candidate, by party identification and education (%)

	Party regardless	Party & candidate	Candidate regardless	Don't vote
Party identification				
Conservative	57	26	6	9
Labour	62	25	4	8
Liberal Democrat	42	42	6	10
Education				
Degree	43	40	6	10
No qualifications	55	24	5	15

Source: British Social Attitudes, 1994

The involved elector

The Maud Committee survey (1965) was concerned to some extent to discover who were the potential councillors, and to that end sought to identify 'the community-conscious elector'. No subsequent inquiry into local government has explored attitudes to giving help to others in the community, despite this being recognised as a route into community service as a locally elected representative. Subsequent studies have instead focused on the common ground of measuring involvement in local organisations. It is not possible to make a direct comparison with Maud, as that survey defined such groups very widely. Comparison is possible, however, between the 1992 SCPR study and the 1994 BSA study. Table 4.34 shows reasonable consistency in the responses to these two surveys, testifying to rather low levels of community involvement.

Table 4.34 Membership of local organisations (%)

	1992	1994
Current membership of:		
Tenants'/residents' association	7	5
Parent-teachers' association	4	3
School board of governors	1	1
Political party	5	3
Trade union	17	N/A
Parish council	1	1
Neighbourhood council/forum	1	1
Other local groups	9	7

Source: DOE, 1992; British Social Attitudes, 1994

Within these categories, however, there are wide variations in the extent to which people are actually active. For example, the 1992 study found that while 17 per cent were members of trade unions, only 3 per cent claimed to be active. The lowest rate of participation by members of groups was found among tenants' and residents' associations, with just two out of seven claiming active membership. Active members of any of these organisations were more likely to be middle-aged, better qualified, non-manual workers, owner-occupiers and men.

Another regularly used measure of the involved elector is attendance at council meetings. The 1992 study asked whether respondents have ever attended a meeting of a county, borough, district city or parish council or a committee meeting, and for the reason why in those cases where a respondent had done so. Overall, 8 per cent of respondents had attended one or the other local meeting over the last 12 months (excluding meetings in relation to community charge), a rather higher figure than that revealed in a MORI survey six years earlier. Respondents were also asked if they had ever attended a public meeting on a local issue; 9 per cent had done so, with a higher proportion of non-manual workers, the middle aged and better qualified and owner-occupiers attending. A comparable question in the 1994 BSA survey produced similar responses.

The potential councillor

People who are active in local affairs may be regarded as a potential pool from which councillors might be drawn. The Maud study (1965), by far the most comprehensive of its type, defined potential councillors as people who possess the following characteristics: a positive view of councillors and their motivations; a positive attitude to the local electoral system; and a strong sense of community responsibility, as measured both by their attitudes and by their involvement in local organisations.

On these measures, only a minority of respondents can be considered as potential councillors. Of them, however, even fewer will have actually stood for election or considered doing so. Maud found that 8 per cent of the respondents to that survey intended to stand, or might stand if the opportunity arose, while 6 per cent had considered doing so and 2 per cent had actually stood. Comparing these figures with the responses to the 1994 BSA study, we found that about 1 per cent (22 respondents) had stood for election in the past, and a further 4 per cent had considered standing but had not done so. This later study did not explore future intentions. So there is some indication here too of a falling-off of interest in participation in local politics. However, with differences in study design intruding upon these very small numbers, the safest judgement might be that nothing much has changed over three decades.

Table 4.35 Attitudes towards becoming a councillor (%)

Have stood	1
Considered, but not stood	4
Not considered	93
Disqualified	2

Source: British Social Attitudes, 1994

The 1994 BSA survey did probe some underlying attitudes which might have some bearing upon the predisposition to consider council service. These included such statements as:

People like me can have a real influence on politics if they are prepared to get involved.

I feel I could do as good a job as councillor as most other people.

Both statements received positive responses from around a third of those interviewed, but, as Table 4.35 shows, the numbers who have actually stood and considered standing are too small to permit any explorations of this possible relationship.

If so few people actively consider service as a councillor, why might this be? In the Maud study, (1965) the great majority of respondents who said they would never wish to stand for election to the local council (88 per cent) were asked to state their reasons. These ranged widely, but the predominant reasons were that they felt insufficiently confident to play the councillor's role (32 per cent), had insufficient time (23 per cent), were too old or in ill-health (13 per cent), or lacked interest (12 per cent). Although a direct comparison would have been invaluable, these questions were not put to the respondents in 1994. Instead, they were asked the indirect – and arguably less satisfactory – question as to why they thought people commonly did not stand. Table 4.36 shows the distribution of responses for what the respondents suppose to be the most common reasons.

Table 4.36 Perceptions of others' reluctance to become councillors (%)

	'Very' or 'fairly' common reasons
Agree ...	
Doesn't occur to them	82
No time to stand	81
Don't have the skills	79
Not enough support	74
Too much party politics	70
Cannot afford	67
Local government has too little power	64

Source: British Social Attitudes, 1994

Conclusion: the value of attitude studies

The foregoing sections of this paper summarise the principal findings of some of the major national public attitude surveys of local government issues which have been carried out in Britain since the pathbreaking Maud Committee inquiry in 1965. What then is to be learned about the value of attitude studies themselves from this exercise?

First, we have seen that matters of factual knowledge are fairly easily addressed by social surveys. The awareness and knowledge questions used in a long series of studies have worked well and proved a reliable measure of awareness and knowledge, with strong inter-survey consistency. The sources of variation are generally unsurprising: the better educated, and those in their middle years return the highest scores. Other circumstances also have a bearing, for example where heads of households proved themselves better informed about the rating system than others.

It is because these measures of knowledge do seem to work well that any trend revealed should be taken seriously. With rising proportions securing high educational qualifications, knowledge levels might be expected to have risen over the last 30 years. The converse is probably true, suggesting that the larger local authorities created in 1972 are less well understood and less accurately perceived than their predecessors, this effect being exacerbated by the presence of a county council. Support for this explanation is to be found in the generally high scores recorded by London and others living in the post-1986 'single-tier' areas.[29] Surveys, then, provide a useful tool for measuring *knowledge*.

It is in the measurement of people's *satisfaction* with their local authorities that the problems inherent in attitude surveys come most into play. These problems are threefold, and concern the spatial scale of service variation, the varying salience of services between different social groups, and the contamination of general satisfaction responses by other, irrelevant, influences.

The first problem concerns the difficulty of tapping variations in satisfaction at the level at which variations in service are likely to occur. Questions about the respondent's level of satisfaction must be understood as addressing his or her subjective experience of local government. That experience will be shaped by the respondent's personal characteristics, by contact with local authorities, by acquaintance with their services, and by variations in the actual provision of those services. Many of those variations will occur at a micro-level – for example the actual quality of street lighting around the resident's home or along some important route travelled at night. Others will occur at the level of the local authority; some authorities simply provide better services than others with respect to (say) libraries or the quality of housing. Aggregating responses across larger areas 'washes out' these variations, and may make large-scale comparisons between authorities of a single type meaningless.

It is only sensible, then, to limit enquiry into the degree of satisfaction with local services to the level at which they might be expected to vary. Examples are to be found in the series of MORI surveys for individual local authorities, in which breakdowns of the responses may be given at ward level. By way of illustration, Table 4.37 is taken from the 1993 MORI study of the London Borough of Tower Hamlets, the purpose of which was to explore differences at the larger-scale neighbourhood level. It abstracts just one of a series of measures of satisfaction with local services – the condition of pavements – chosen as a measure of something which all residents experience more or less equally, and which are known to vary at a micro-level. Even here, however, the results provide only the roughest indication of responses to actual variations.

Table 4.37 Satisfaction with the condition of pavements: Tower Hamlets Neighbourhoods (%)

	'Very' or 'fairly' satisfied
Bow	55
Bethnal green	52
Globetown	52
Isle of Dogs	41
Poplar	38
Stepney	50
Wapping	58

Source: MORI, 1994

The second problem arises from the common conflation of those who use, and those who do not use, certain kinds of service. More robust conclusions can be drawn in relation to other services by distinguishing between those respondents who have contact with, or use, a particular service and those who do not, confining the measurement of satisfaction to the former by means of filter questions. This device goes some way to exclude meaningless responses from either national or local surveys, although it may also be useful to compare the satisfaction levels of users and non-users where it is suspected that the latter might find existing services hard to access.

The third problem with satisfaction studies is to be found in the propensity of responses to questions about satisfaction with local government to be shaped by satisfaction with other life-domains. It is well known that responses to questions about satisfaction with national government are greatly coloured by the extent to which the respondent supports or opposes the governing party. So too in local government, where the 1985 Widdicombe and 1990 JRF surveys showed sharp differences in satisfaction according to whether or not respondents were 'politically sympathetic' to the local council; Conservatives living in Conservative-controlled areas were found to be about ten percentage points more satisfied than Conservatives living elsewhere.

By extension, variations among social groups are patterned in such a way as to suggest that their reported satisfaction with their local council is actually driven by other factors which are themselves irrelevant to local government. The young (in these surveys) are more satisfied than the middle aged and old, men more than women, owner-occupiers more than council tenants, higher social class groups more than lower, those living outside metropolitan England more than those in the conurbations. We are led to suspect that highly general and non-specific 'satisfaction with the local council' questions may actually be tapping a still more general *satisfaction with life* dimension. Those with power, hope, opportunity, and a better quality of life appear more satisfied with their local councils – and doubtless much else besides. Such questions may tell us no more than who is happy, and who is not.

With these considerations in mind, then, we might conclude that the most commonly-used questions in surveys of attitudes to local government may be the least useful. But are the surveys themselves of value? We think so. The understandable concern to evaluate councils has propelled the increasing use of attitude surveys, and provided a valuable political tool in expanding notions of accountability. And while local surveys have an immediate utility, when considered in the aggregate they can go beyond that to provide a wider picture of life in Britain today.[30] There also remains much of value to be learned from more broadly-conceived studies, in particular from those national surveys which have ranged widely across the field of local democracy. We would argue for the continuation of such studies at suitable intervals, with particular attention paid to the repetition of earlier successful questions. In this way we might obtain a running 'health check' on the state of local democracy.

Notes

1. Local Government Management Board in association with MORI, *Employee Attitudes to Local Government*, Luton, January 1994.

2. For a rare example of an attempt to ascertain those views systematically, see G. Jones and T. Travers, *Attitudes to Local Government in Westminster and Whitehall*, London, Commission for Local Democracy, 1994.

3. N. Rao, *The Making and Un-making of Local Self-government*, Aldershot, Gower, 1994; K. Young and N. Rao, *Coming to Terms with Change? The Local Government Councillor in 1993*, York, Joseph Rowntree Foundation, 1994.

4. W. Miller, M. Dickson and I. Murray, 'Attitudes to local governance', unpublished summary paper made available by the author.

5. J. Herwald Morris, *Local Government Areas*, London, Shaw and Sons, 1960, pp. 49–50.

6. J. March, 'Local government meets the structure review', *Municipal Journal*, vol. 45, 12–18 November 1993, pp. 14–15. K. Young, *People, Places and Power: Community Identity and Local Democracy*, Belgrave Paper No. 8, Luton, Local Government Management Board, 1993. Although it is not intended that further studies should be commissioned, even by the affected authorities themselves, the existing survey evidence will be given due weight in considering proposals put to the Commission; see Department of the Environment, *Policy and Procedure Guidance to the Local Government Commission for England*, June 1995.

7. Newcastle City Council, *West City Consumer Survey 1985: First Report: The Use of Public Services and Consumer Attitudes to the Local Authority of Newcastle*, 1985; Market and Opinion Research International, *1987 Residents' Attitudes Survey: January–February 1987*, London, MORI, February 1987.

8. See Harris Research Centre, *Survey of Public Opinion in London*, June 1983; Market Opinion and Research International, *Attitudes of Londoners to the Abolition of the GLC, 7–9 July 1984: Research Study Conducted for the Greater London Council*, London, MORI, 1984. For discussion of similar use of public attitudes as evidence against the abolition of the GLC's provincial equivalents, see C. Game, 'Public attitudes to the abolition of the mets', *Local Government Studies*, vol. 13, no. 5, September–October 1987, pp. 12–130, and the same author's 'Public attitudes to metropolitan government', *Local Government Studies*, vol. 16, no. 3, May–June 1990, pp. 47–67.

9. Although responses to the surveys carried out by MORI, the market leaders in this field, tend to be aggregated up to local authority level, the questions asked are generally closely focused upon local government as it is experienced in the respondent's own neighbourhood. This goes some way to mitigate the problems inherent in such questions.

10. Committee on the Management of Local Government, *Volume 3: The Local Government Elector*, London, HMSO, 1967 (hereafter 'Maud, 1965').

11. Committee of Inquiry into the Conduct of Local Authority Business, *Research Volume III: The Local Government Elector*, Cmnd 9800, London, HMSO, 1986 (hereafter 'Widdicombe, 1985'). In between the 1965 and 1985 surveys, the Redcliffe-Maud Commission surveyed the more limited issue of community attitudes.

12. A. Bloch and P. John, *Attitudes to Local Government*, York, Joseph Rowntree Foundation, 1990 (hereafter 'JRF, 1990').

13. P. Lynn, *Public Perceptions of Local Government*, London, HMSO, 1992 (hereafter 'DoE, 1992').

14. K. Young and N. Rao, 'Faith in local democracy', in R. Jowell and J. Curtice (eds), *British Social Attitudes: the Twelfth Report*, Aldershot, Gower, 1995 (hereafter 'BSA, 1994).

15. See Widdicombe, *The Local Government Elector*, p. 30.

16. The JRF study, which was itself largely modelled on Widdicombe for purposes of comparison, provided the simplest account of general knowledge, awarding points for each correct response to questions on structure, party control and responsibility for council services, to produce a two-category classification. The Widdicombe survey's four categories ('well informed', 'quite well informed', not very well informed' and 'uninformed') were similarly derived, and were collapsed into two categories. The study conducted by SCPR for the DoE did not ask about knowledge of services for this purpose, including instead more questions on knowledge of the sources of local finance. The four-part categorisation introduced in the Widdicombe study was adopted, and despite the slight differences in the content of the items making up the scores, the overall pattern is judged to be similar (DoE, 1992, p. 11).

17. National Consumer Council, *Consumer Concerns 1995: A Consumer View of Council Services*, London, NCC, August 1995.

18. The NCC's 1995 report refers to a programme of studies undertaken for the Council by MORI since 1991, but occasional references are made to figures drawn from a 1986 survey for which no further details are given.

19. G. Almond and S. Verba, *The Civic Culture: Political Attitudes and Democracy in Five Nations*, Princeton NJ, Princeton University Press, 1963. See also the same authors' edited volume, *The Civic Culture Revisited*, Boston, Little Brown, 1980.

20. It has also provided for some misinterpretation of those findings and subsequent use of the same question, leading some to overestimate the degree of culture change that occurred between 1960 and 1984. See, for example, R. Topf, 'Political change and political culture in Britain, 1959–87', in J.R. Gribbins (ed.), *Contemporary Political Culture: Politics in a Postmodern Age*, London, Sage, 1990, pp. 52–80. The important point, missed by Topf, is that the 1960 question was open-ended; findings were presented for the most common responses which have since formed the basis of fixed-choice questions.

21. Market and Opinion Research International, *Tower Hamlets Residents Survey: Research Carried out for Tower Hamlets Council*, January 1994, London, MORI.

22. For an examination of attitudes to the representative role of local councillors, see N. Rao, 'Representation in local politics: a reconsideration and some new evidence', *Political Studies*, forthcoming, 1997.

23. For a discussion, see M. Goldsmith, *Options for the Future: Local Government Abroad*, Luton, LGMB, 1992.

24. Lynn, *Public Perceptions of Local Government*, p. 48. A fairly complete discussion of the effect of these factors is to be found in Maud, *The Local Government Elector*, pp. 78–9.

25. The first of the statements considered here appears to reflect a judgement about the meaningfulness of local elections, while the second – and especially the third – probably also reflect something of the individual's own sense of powerlessness.

26. Maud, *The Local Government Elector*, p. 69.

27. There may also be a previously unnoticed question effect in the wording of the question itself, which could imply, to the less knowledgeable respondent, that in most areas all councillors come from a single political party, a position which, if true, is still less likely to be generally acceptable.

28. The measure used here gives only an approximate indicator of rurality. It summarises population density per hectare at the most localised level, and therefore probably understates the effects of more or less urbanised local authorities.

29. Bloch and John, *Attitudes to Local Government*, pp. 9–10.

30. For a Rowntree-funded attempt to use a large number of similarly designed local surveys to build a national picture, see K. Young, W. Hatter and B. Gosschalk, *In Search of Community Identity*, York, Joseph Rowntree Foundation, 1996.

Local political participation
Gerry Stoker

Introduction

This paper reviews recent research about local political participation. It follows Parry *et al.* (1992, p. 16) and adopts a broad definition of political participation as 'taking part in the processes of formulation, passage and implementation of public policies'. Broad as this definition is, it does focus on participation in relation to governmental activities and on actions which are aimed at influencing decision-making. Seen in this light, participation nevertheless refers to a range of activities. Voting, contacting an elected representative, canvassing for a political party, signing a petition, attending a protest meeting, joining a pressure group or going on a demonstration march could all count as examples of local political participation. Participation therefore requires a range of skills and commitment and in its various forms is likely to generate different degrees of conflict.

Participation would seem fundamental to the operation of democratic government. Most acts of participation are directed towards those in authority and who are able to influence decisions. Those in authority may, in addition, seek participation to supplement their decision-making. Yet there remains a debate about how much participation is appropriate. Theorists of democracy disagree about the extent of popular participation they would consider desirable. Most, however, would argue that in Western democracies participation should be voluntary rather than compulsory. People should choose whether and how to get involved.

The evolution of participation
As a policy issue in political debate, participation gained prominence in the 1960s in Britain and in other Western democracies. Two factors are often identified as underlying the rise of participation to the status of political slogan. First, the post-war increase in material standards had, it was argued, created the conditions for a new political activism based on post-materialist values. Second, the expansion of the activities of the state had created a wider context for a range of citizen demands and protests. Local government became caught up in these general trends (Hill, 1970). The new mood of official interest in participation, for example, was expressed through the Skeffington Report and the establishment of Community Development Projects in 1969. The 1960s and

early 1970s saw increased mobilisation by community and tenants' groups within local politics (Hain, 1980).

Interest in participation undoubtedly declined in the 1980s at the height of the New Right agenda. From its viewpoint, reforming local government was more a matter of introducing market forces or market-like mechanisms into public services rather than promoting citizen participation as such. The consumer rather than the citizen was to be sovereign. However, the citizen as consumer was to be encouraged in some elements of direct participation as in the case of, for example, parents on governing bodies. Local authorities, too, responded to the pressure to be more consumer-sensitive by developing techniques of market research, consumer feedback and consultation.

The context for the debate about participation in the 1990s is rather different. Mulgan (1994) speculates about three characteristics of today's politics. First, there is a search for individual meaning and identity reflecting the loss of much of the cultural homogeneity that bound together interests in the past. Second, there is the continuing questioning of the role of the state and its functions, legitimacy and competence. Third, there is the rise of a global public which challenges traditional notions of sovereignty and the boundaries of politics. These three factors play out in the context of extensive disenchantment with politics. A study undertaken for Lancashire County Council (Macnaughton, 1995) based on small panel discussions found 'pervasive feelings of distrust and cynicism towards public institutions, including national and local government'. Reviewing more conventional opinion survey evidence, Curtice and Jowell (1995, p. 167) conclude 'British people have clearly become less trusting of their politicians and political institutions in the last two decades. They are also more sceptical about the ability of the system to respond to the demands of the citizenry.'

Broad generalisations about participation in the 1960s compared to the 1990s need to be treated with caution. The survey evidence available from the 1960s suggests that public interest and confidence in the local political process was not all that deep (Horton, 1967; Royal Commission, 1969) and in the subsequent 30 or so years has remained at a modest level. There never was a golden age of participation with respect to local government.

Participation as a device in policy-making is no longer seen as a panacea. However, it has sustained its place on the policy agenda. If anything, with the rethinking of the role of local government and the broader debate about local democracy reflected in, for example, the report by the Commission for Local Democracy, the 1990s has seen a revival of interest in participation.

The structure of the report

Firstly, evidence about the extent of participation is provided. This is followed by a discussion of the general trends in participation over the last 30 years and an examination of the current range of debates about the role of participation in local politics. Then evidence is examined on voting in local elections, the basic participatory act. The report looks at the variety of officially sponsored participation schemes and goes on to look at participation trends beyond the state and, in particular, examines evidence on social movements and third force organisations. This is followed by a consideration of the research that has been conducted into experimental forms of participation. Each of the main sections of the report concludes with an overview of the state of research and a brief consideration of the policy implications of core findings from research. The final section of the report provides a general commentary on future research priorities with respect to local political participation.

Who participates?

The extent of involvement

Hague *et al.* (1992, p. 157) comment that 'the most striking fact about political participation in liberal democracies is how little of it there is'. Britain among Western democracies would in the past have been seen as having one of the least participatory cultures, yet a major study conducted for the ESRC and published in 1992 lays out a basic 'cartography' of political action in Britain which indicates a substantial scale and range of participation. Moreover, much of that participation is directed towards and takes place at the local level. To gain a baseline understanding of participation the ESRC study provides an excellent starting point (see Parry *et al.*, 1992).

The ESRC study draws its initial evidence from a national sample survey of nearly 1600 people. The data gives information on people's reporting of their participation activities and provides a reasonable base from which to allow a range of inferences to be made about the participation habits of the British population as a whole. The survey work was conducted in the mid-1980s and people were asked about their political activity over the previous five years. Voting and signing a petition emerged as the most widely claimed political activities from the list of 23 assembled by Parry *et al.* (1992). Contacting a councillor and visiting the town hall to raise an issue were activities claimed in each case by about a fifth of the sample. Group activity of an informal and formal nature were claimed by 13.8 and 11.2 per cent of the sample. Attending a protest meeting was an activity identified by 15 per cent of the sample. Party-based campaigning was not a very popular activity. Involvement in violent or highly disruptive political acts such as blocking traffic with a street demonstration were also the preserve of a very small minority of the population.

Table 5.1 Types of political participation in Britain

	% of population
Just voters	51.0
Almost inactives	25.8
Activitists	23.2
Collective	(8.7)
Contacting	(7.7)
Direct	(3.1)
Party	(2.2)
Complete	(1.5)
	100.0

Source: Parry et al. (1992)

Participation of an extensive nature is a minority activity. Based on their research material Parry *et al.* (1992, p. 228) divide the population into three broad camps (see Table 5.1). The largest group, comprising just over half the population, is composed of those who just vote but do so very regularly. Their other participatory acts tend to be relatively infrequent and spasmodic. The other half of the population is split into two very different camps. About a quarter of the population might be regarded as 'almost inactive' and did not even report voting very regularly. The other quarter constitute the activists. They had engaged in a range and variety of political participation in the previous five years.

Defining only a quarter of the population as activists may cause dismay since the vast majority would then appear to be either passive or disaffected. On the other hand Parry *et al.* (1992, pp. 22–3) estimate that, translated into population numbers, their study indicates nearly ten million people could be seen as relatively participatory – a number large enough to make some government officials worry!

Parry *et al.* (1992) make clear that where the participatory minority is engaged it is concerned on the whole with local matters. The activism that they identified is concerned with planning proposals, the availability of council housing, school closures and other local issues. Much of this activism is directed towards those in authority in their locality.

The pattern of limited participation revealed by Parry *et al.* (1992) is confirmed in complementary findings from other recent studies. In particular, two survey-based studies funded by the Department of the Environment investigated involvement in local affairs. Lynn (1992, Chapters 10 and 11) found that a quarter of respondents expressed a great deal or fair amount of interest in local politics. The remaining three-quarters said they had either not much or no interest at all. Overall one in seven respondents said they were active members of a group such as a tenants' association, school governing body, local community organisation. About two-thirds of respondents said they would take action if their council proposed something they strongly disapproved of. Young and Rao (1995) too asked respondents whether they were members of different kinds of local voluntary groups such as a residents' association or a local conservation group. They found that just over a quarter of their sample said they were a member of at least one organisation. Neighbourhood Watch schemes topped the list as a participatory activity. Involvement in party political activity was very much a minority activity.

The variety of activists
One of the interesting features of the ESRC study is that it demonstrates that activism has a pluralistic character. What distinguishes the activists one from another is the nature of their specialism. Parry *et al.* (1992) identify five different types of activist (see Table 5.1). The contacting activists were people who made their own path to the authorities by contacting a councillor, MP, or by going to the media or the town hall to raise an issue of concern. The collective activists were those where most of reported participatory activity involved working in support of an organised or informal campaigning group. Taken together, the contacting and collective activists constituted over two-thirds of the activist group. The direct activists were characterised by their willingness to engage in more confrontational or protest-style activism. The party campaigners engaged in party-based activity. The complete campaigners not only engaged in party activity but extended their efforts to other spheres as well. These last three groups constituted minority elements in the activist group.

The evidence produced by Parry *et al.* (1992, Table 10.3, p. 234) reveals that activists on the whole tend to be better educated, wealthier, better networked and are more likely to be members of the salariat (i.e. managers, professionals, etc.) than the total population. On closer examination, however, each group of activists has a distinctive social profile.

Activists are not representative of the population but they are not comprehensively the largely middle-class, educated and better-off sub-set that might be expected. Party and complete activists fall predominantly into such a category. Contacting and collective activists draw a roughly proportionate element of the working class. They tend to draw from better educated and wealthier sections of the population but not to the same extent as the party and complete activists. Direct activists have a substantial working-class base and are less wealthy and lack formal qualifications compared to other activist categories. Men make up a disproportionate share of the contacting, direct and complete activists. Women take a greater share of collective and party activists.

Local variation

To investigate the local political scene further Parry (1992) and his colleagues undertook a sample survey of 1600 people and 300 leaders in six selected localities. The six localities were:

- Sevenoaks - a medium-sized town in Kent

- Penrhiwceiber - a mining village in South Wales

- Stockwell - an inner city area in Lambeth

- Spotland - an area near the centre of Rochdale

- Oswestry - a market town in Shropshire

- The Machar - a rural community in South West Scotland

A sample of the population in each locality was asked about its participatory activity.

With respect to citizen mobilisation Parry and his colleagues found local variations sufficient enough to suggest that there were local participatory effects worth investigating. Machars and Oswestry emerge in a broad sense as the least participatory. Sevenoaks and Stockwell are the most participatory. Further analysis reveals something more than a compositional effect at work. Sevenoaks has a level of participation which matches expectations given the resources and values of its citizens. Penrhiwceiber and Stockwell have greater levels of participation than might be expected given their social composition. These are relatively modest deviations from underlying patterns, yet Parry et al. (1992) suggest that there is some evidence of a locality effect. Participation patterns and trends in the localities reflect what might be expected given the different social profiles of the areas but there is a strong indication that in different areas local leadership, culture and organisations can enhance the propensity of citizens to participate.

Conclusions

The ESRC study by Parry *et al.* (1992) reveals that the nature of participants engaged in political action is more complex than is sometimes understood. Only a select group of highly educated, articulate and well-resourced individuals are complete activists but nearly a quarter of the population would appear to engage in substantial activism. People appear to have a predilection for certain types of actions. Different participants emerge with distinctive social profiles. Parry *et al.* (1992, p. 237) conclude:

> *Those who would call for a more participatory form of political life might perhaps heed its pluralist character. It may be the case that there will never be more than a relatively small group of complete activists. But this is not to say that, in the right conditions, far more people might not find time and opportunity to contact their representatives to press an issue, or to campaign for a party, or join in a pressure group or, if necessary, take to the streets. These are all ways in which a variety of people with a range of abilities and a plurality of goals can keep the authorities on their toes. There is no single avenue for participation and a society of participatory 'specialists' can have much to commend it.*

At this point it is worth introducing different perspectives on politics which provide the basis for debate on local political participation.

Why participate?

Instrumental perspective

The first, and a widely held view, is that politics is about expressing and defending interests. Participation is about the promotion of participants' goals with the maximum of effect and the minimum of costs. In order to participate, people might be seen to require a certain sense of confidence or efficacy. They might also be expected to make 'rational' calculations to assess the value of their involvement.

This instrumental perspective on participation might be seen as encouraging a realist understanding of the issues. People will participate if a relevant issue comes up and if they believe their intervention will be effective. Participation will tend to be an activity in which only a small portion of the population are extensively involved. The majority will engage in only spasmodic intervention. A lack of intensity of interest and a realistic assessment of the power constraints they face discourage many citizens from a more active role. What is important is that there are mechanisms so that where major concerns exist sufficient numbers of the population believe that their mobilisation can change matters. 'The so-called realists do not, therefore, measure the health of a liberal democracy by the high levels of involvement by the citizenry but, rather, by the stability of the system and by its capacity to permit checks on the leaders' (Parry *et al.*, 1992, p. 5).

The survey evidence reviewed in the first section of this report could from a realist perspective be seen as not too problematic. A limited number of activists is to be expected and what is clear is that people still appear willing to mobilise over issues that are of concern. Young and Rao (1995) suggest that in the mid-1990s substantial numbers of people (roughly two-fifths) appear to remain confident they could have a real influence on local politics if they were prepared to get involved. Within the limits of people's interest and resource capacity, it could be argued, local political participation is in as healthy a state as it ever was.

Many radical critics share an instrumental understanding of participation with the realists. They are, however, less sanguine about public apathy. For them participation is about power and ability of different interests to achieve what they want. Power will depend on information, money and other resources. The non-mobilisation of substantial elements of the public reflects the unequal distribution of the capacity to act. Participation where it is officially sponsored is conducted on the terms of the powerful. Boaden *et al.* (1982, p. 179), for example, conclude a review of local public participation initiatives since the 1960s: 'In the end, elite perspectives have won out, and participation has served the purposes of building up a consensus for the proposals of those in power, thereby legitimating them.'

Participatory perspective

The classic alternative perspective to that of the realists is taken by those who see democracy as requiring the maximum possible participation by the citizen. Two sources of thinking tend to underlie this perspective. One view – a communitarian perspective – stresses that involvement in politics is not a matter of instrumental calculation but is rather about a concern for the collective, the community of which a person is part. A second view stresses the value of participation as an educative experience. By taking part in politics, people gain in terms of their own self-development, competence and confidence. In addition, they come to more fully appreciate the interests and aspirations of their fellows. 'A more participatory society would be one which was more likely to be integrated and trusting' (Parry *et al.*, 1992, p. 14).

This participatory perspective is prone to see a special virtue in local government and politics. John Stuart Mill is well known for his advocacy of local government as an arena in which citizenship and politics can be developed. Its accessibility and very 'localness' make it an ideal base for citizen participation. It provides a forum for exploring community interests and drawing people into the world of politics in a way that enables them to learn and grow. The tone of such arguments can have a somewhat patronising flavour, yet at their heart they remain concerned with participation as a means to self-realisation and the expression of community concern.

The survey evidence reviewed in the previous section gives the advocates of maximum participation some cause for concern. Citizen participation and interest is limited. Yet where people do participate they tend to do so at the local level. There are signs of hope in the differential capacity for mobilisation displayed in various communities. The organisation of politics appears to make a difference so there may be scope to increase participation. Finally, survey evidence shows that among the population there is sympathy for the ideal that local government should be reformed to allow citizens more say in decision-making (see Dunleavy and Weir, 1994; Dickson *et al.*, 1995).

There are other currents in the debate about the virtues of local participation that also need to be considered. The debate in the 1960s was, in a broad sense, between the realists who tended to defend existing arrangements of representative government at the local level, and the Utopian vision of the advocates of maximum participation and more direct forms of democracy. In the 1990s the fundamental opposition between these positions has not gone away but the debate has been made more complex by other currents. It is possible to identify two elements: a politics of presence and a politics of deliberation.

Politics of presence

The politics of presence is premised on the demands of excluded groups to be involved in decision-making. As Phillips (1995, p. 5) comments:

> *Many of the current arguments over democracy revolve around what we might call demands for political presence: demands for the equal representation of women with men; demands for a more even-handed balance between the different ethnic groups that make up each society; demands for the political inclusion of groups that have come to see themselves as marginalised or silenced or excluded.*

The demand is not simply that their views are taken into account; it is that they should be represented in politics by people who share their experience and identity.

Presence, it is argued, provides a challenge to existing patterns of exclusion and marginalisation in a number of ways. First there is a symbolic value in having members of the excluded group present at the decision-making table. Representatives must not only be representative but they must be seen to be so. As Parry *et al.* (1992, p. 15) note, participation can be expressive: people act to express their feelings and their identity. Yet, as Phillips (1995) argues, the politics of presence – as perceived by, for example, the women's movement or some disabled people's organisations – rests on the assumption that the direct presence of representatives of their group makes a difference to decision-making outcomes. It opens the decision-making process and creates the conditions for a more vigorous advocacy of their interests. It further facilitates a politics of transformation by giving previously excluded groups the time and opportunity to construct their political preferences and express their concerns for themselves.

Deliberative democracy

A strand in the debates about participation that has a greater prominence in the 1990s compared to the 1960s is the politics of deliberation. This view is critical of instrumental and presence arguments for participation as being too focused on self-interest. It differs from the advocates of direct democracy in not seeing maximum participation as necessary a good thing in itself. Fishkin (1991, p. 53), for example, rejects the advocacy of participation for its own sake and argues that it is to be prized when it is instrumental in the creation of political institutions that deliver political equality and deliberation. The advocates of deliberative democracy do, however, tend to favour widespread public participation (see Barber, 1984; Cohen, 1989). Yet they are critical of political structures which see politics in instrumental terms, a battle of interests in which the task of government is to strike a balance between different demands. Political institutions need rather to be designed to enable citizens to relate to each other as deliberators or reason-givers and not simply as bargainers engaged in exchange. Above all, the advocates of deliberative democracy suggest that politics should involve reasoning, open debate and reflection on the opinions of others. Indeed, while most do not necessarily see in a simplistic way the emergence of a 'common good', they all hold to the view that during the course of deliberation new positions and understandings will emerge. Participation structured in a deliberative way will lead to new solutions and better decision-making.

Rationales for participation

To conclude, it is clear that the rationale for participation can vary. From a citizen perspective, participation can be seen as instrumental, a civic duty, expressive or deliberative. Figure 5.1 expresses this argument in terms of two dimensions: the intensity of an individuals' participation and the nature of participants' motivation.

Figure 5.1 Rationales for participation

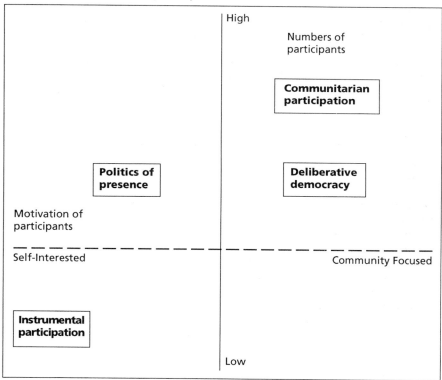

The issue can be seen in instrumental terms. Participation can be seen as a means of individuals achieving their goals. They will participate if they care enough about an issue and if it is worth the effort. Most of the time people will remain inactive. For some, such apathy reflects a lack of intense interest. For others it reflects a lack of political power. Others see participation as something to be valued in itself. It expresses a concern for the community of which you are part and provides an opportunity for learning the art of citizenship. These respectively 'instrumental' and 'communitarian' perspectives occupy diagonally opposite segments of Figure 5.1. The advocates of a politics of presence see participation by representatives of excluded groups as important for symbolic and instrumental reasons. It demonstrates the inclusion of that group and its interests and it provides a better environment for those interests to be advanced. Not all members of the group have to be actively engaged in political activity but the presence of representatives in the decision-making arena with whom they can identify and who have shared their experience, facilitates the expression of their group interest. Those who support participation, but structured in a way to maximise deliberation, offer another perspective. Participation as such is not valued by them. Their overriding objective is the creation of a deliberative polity in which people exchange views, reformulate their understanding and develop shared solutions. A limited range and variety of people should be drawn into participation in a manner that encourages deliberation. The politics of presence and deliberative participation on this basis occupy different upper quadrants of Figure 5.1.

Local voting and non-voting

The value of local voting

Debates about participation in local government sometimes neglect voting and concentrate on other forms of participation. Yet voting plays a vital role in democracy. As Phillips (1994, p. 16) comments:

> *Whichever way we see it, its greatest claim in terms of democracy is that it offers all voters an equal chance to decide on the people to represent them. It relies, that is, on what is the most commonly exercised form of political involvement, and it makes no excessive demands on political energy and time.*

Voting provides a low cost mechanism for citizens to hold governmental agencies to account.

How much faith do the public have in local elections? This question is central to the analysis developed by Ken Young and Nirmala Rao as part of the British

Social Attitudes Survey for 1994. Young and Rao (1995, pp. 9–11) found that there had been a substantial decline in the proportion of people who think that voting in local elections decides what goes on in their area.

Table 5.2 Trends in attitudes towards local elections

% who agree that	1965 %	1985 %	1994 %
The way that people vote in local elections is the main thing that decides how things are run in this area	77	60	54
Local council election are sometimes so complicated that I really don't know who to vote for	29	34	30

Note: 1965 figure is from research for the Maud Committee (Horton, 1967) and the 1985 figure is from research for the Widdicombe Committee (Young, 1986).

As Table 5.2 shows, people do not think that elections have become more complicated but only just over half, compared to three-quarters 30 years ago, believe that local elections decide things. Among young people, between the ages of 18 and 24, only 41 per cent felt that local elections are the main thing that decides things in the area. This same group was more prone to seeing local elections as complicated. Further, those with educational qualifications and people living in urban areas are less likely, on average, to have confidence in the efficacy of local elections. Overall, however, the same survey did find that just over half the population disagreed with the proposition that 'there is no point in voting in local elections because in the end it makes no difference who gets in'.

One interesting and consistent finding from surveys is that more people claim to vote in local elections than would appear to do so in practice. Lynn (1992, pp. 48–50), for example, found that nearly two-thirds said they had voted in the last local election and a roughly similar proportion claimed they were certain or very likely to vote in future local elections. Rallings and Thrasher (1994, p. 5), using their large-scale set of results, found overall turnout at local elections since 1973 to average approximately 40 per cent and to vary little by authority type. Indeed, they suggest that there has been a slight increase in turnout since 1973. Claimed voting, however, would appear to be running ahead of actual voting.

The same apparent over-reporting of voting has been found in earlier studies (see Miller, 1986, p. 124). Lynn (1992, p. 48) suggests that three factors might help explain the observed discrepancy. First, people who agree to participate in a survey may be more likely to vote. Second, people may be reluctant to admit that they do not vote. Finally, it may be that actual turnout figures are flawed because of inaccuracies and misinformation contained on the electoral register. On the last point, Rallings *et al.* (1994, p. 25) indicate that, if anything, the quality of electoral registers has improved in recent years although there is some evidence that the poll tax may have led to some under-registration.

To continue to explore local voting requires that two questions are addressed: How do voters make their choice at local elections and, in particular, do local issues or national politics determine voting patterns? What factors explain non-voting?

Local and non-local influences on voting

It is common in the media to treat local elections as a test of the parties at national level. Some academic support for this position is found in Newton's (1976) study of Birmingham's local elections between 1945 and 1965. Newton found that 'no more than 10 per cent of the variance in Birmingham election results may be attributable to local factors' (pp. 14–15). Indeed, Newton (1976, p.16) goes on to argue:

> In fact, the term 'local election' is something of a misnomer, for there is very little that is local about them, and they tell us practically nothing about the preferences and attitudes of citizens to purely local issues and events. They are determined overwhelmingly by national political considerations. Local elections are a sort of annual general election.

The main thrust of research produced since Newton's strongly expressed analysis has been to suggest that local factors have a stronger impact than he suggests. Indeed it may be that the political intensity of local government has increased since the period on which Newton focused. What does more recent analysis indicate?

The most substantial study is provided by Miller (1986 pp. 166–70) in work initially undertaken for the Widdicombe Committee in the mid-1980s. Using a survey conducted in 1985 he found that local election choices were very strongly determined by party identification and even more strongly determined by current national voting preferences. In total, four-fifths of local voters vote exactly in accord with their national party identification or current national preference. The slippage between national and local choice reflected the finding that some electors do not have a national choice and some are more willing to vote for 'third' parties and other candidates in local elections. Miller (1986, p. 169) concludes there is 'some scope for the impact of local influences on local voting. Roughly a tenth of local voters do not have a national party identification and another tenth vote out of accord with their national party identification'.

The survey evidence used by Miller (1986, p. 169) did find that over half the electorate claims to vote in local elections on local issues. He also notes that because the survey was conducted in December 1995 – at a time far away from a local election atmosphere – then it may be that the responses over-stressed national partisanship. Others argue that even when voters support candidates of the same party in local and national elections they may also do so on the basis of different considerations (Wilson and Game, 1994, p. 199). Lynn (1992 pp. 50–2) found in a survey undertaken in January–March 1990 that, overall, 40 per cent of respondents 'said that there were some local issues which would be important to them' in deciding how to vote. The proportion saying that local issues were important was higher among the 'upper' socio-economic groups, the better qualified, the middle aged and among owner-occupiers. Environment, education, expenditure and planning were the top four local issues of importance among local voters.

Those seeking to demonstrate the influence of local factors can also point to evidence of split voting in the May 1979 combined general and local elections and in the inconsistency of voting patterns. Wilson and Game (1994, pp. 198–202) review such evidence and comment:

> It is possible to find plenty of evidence of the impact of local electoral influences through a careful study of almost any set of local results. Immediately you start digging beneath the headlines and the aggregated figures, you are almost sure to be struck by the immense diversity and apparent inconsistency of the detailed ward-by-ward results. (p. 200)

Most researchers accept that there is considerable variation around national trends and patterns which does reflect different local influences. Yet even the most ardent of the localists (Jones and Stewart, 1985) accept that national government popularity has a dominant effect upon local elections. As Miller (1986, p. 147) argues, 'the existence of a nation-wide trend does not preclude local trends and variations. The question of local versus national influences is not necessarily an either/or question, it can be both/and.'

Explaining election turnout

The average 40 per cent turnout in British local elections is low by international standards. As Rallings *et al.* (1994, p. 17) demonstrate, the gap is considerable with the next lowest in the European Union league table of average turnout in sub-national elections being the Netherlands at 54 per cent. They also indicate that there is evidence to suggest that Western systems with PR (proportional representation) tend to have higher turnouts than those such as Britain which employ first past the post.

The paper by Rallings *et al.* (1994, pp. 18–21) provides a useful review of case study evidence on factors that may contribute to low turnout in local elections. Party campaigning and activity, the physical closeness of polling booths and the marginality of the seat would all appear to have some positive effect on the willingness of voters to come out. Two other major sources of evidence on non-voting require also to be reviewed.

Miller, again, provides important evidence based on the same 1985 Widdicombe Survey supplemented by a further poll funded by the ESRC. The second poll involved re-interviewing roughly three-quarters of the original 1000-plus Widdicombe sample in May 1986. The results are reported in Miller (1988). The key findings are as follows:

- The electorate is not divided into regular local election voters and regular abstainers.

- In terms of personal characteristics, age and length of residence are correlated to the propensity to vote.

- Having a sense of psychological involvement in politics was also an important factor. Knowledge of and interest in politics and in particular local politics were strongly correlated to the turnout.

Further evidence on non-voting is provided by Rallings and Thrasher (1994) in work funded by the Department of the Environment. Using their substantial aggregate data on local election results they examined the dynamics of turnout. The key findings are as follows:

- The proximity of a general election, perceived or otherwise, has a positive effect on local turnout. So too does the prominence of a major issue such as the poll tax debate in 1990.

- Structural variables such as the size of the council or the nature of its electoral cycle seem to have little impact on turnout.

- Political variables – in particular the closeness of the contest between parties – do appear to have a positive impact on propensity to vote.

- The social-economic character of an area explained more of the variance in turnout than structural/political factors. Local authorities with high unemployment, high levels of council housing and other signs of relative deprivation were particularly prone to record low turnouts.

Rallings *et al.* (1994, p. 28) point out that, notwithstanding the general factors identified by researchers, there is still evidence of electors in certain authorities who defy the trends.

> *Regardless of socio-economic status, regardless of the scale of party competition, regardless of the state of the council and ward marginality, voters in authorities such as Rossendale, Richmond upon Thames and Stockport appear to turn out in greater numbers than we might expect.*

Equally there is evidence of some authorities consistently under-performing. All this suggests that there are other, perhaps local, variables at play as yet unidentified by researchers.

Conclusions
The political act of voting in local elections is in a relatively unhealthy state. People appear to be losing faith in local elections. Although actual turnout levels have not declined they remain low by international standards. Moreover, although not determining elections, national factors do play a major role. There may be few regular abstainers in local elections but there are deep-lying factors related to an individual's sense of political efficacy and socio-economic status that explain non-voting. Political variables relating to the presence of controversy and competition do enhance turnout. Moreover, there are practical issues about the organisation of the election and the closeness of polling booths that would appear to have an influence. Finally, elements of local political culture would also appear to have an effect.

Officially sponsored participation

The scope and limitations of 'official' participation

Participation as a policy device has usually involved attempts at stimulating non-electoral public participation. In many respects such initiatives are an activity central to democratic practice. As Beetham (1996) argues, representative democracy involves participation by citizens as part of a continuous process of exchange. Representation is not captured in the single act of election, it is a process which involves citizens and representatives in mutual sharing and learning. Participation is not an alternative to representative democracy; it is a necessary condition. Yet there is undoubtedly a fear on behalf of some representatives of the claims of more direct public involvement and a sense that the voices of community and other interests are not fully legitimate. Research for the ESRC's Local Governance Programme has tested the views of councillors (based on a sample of nearly 800). It found over two-thirds were in favour of encouraging demand expression or direct participation in the abstract but only just over a sixth felt that community groups were more effective or more representative of local opinion (Dickson *et al.*, 1995, p. 21).

Many advocates of participation are suspicious of the motives of officialdom in promoting participation. Reviewing experience to the early 1980s, Boaden *et al.* (1982, pp. 169–71) argue that élites may favour participation as a legitimating device or as a way of gaining information to improve policies or services, but do not favour participation that involves a shift of power:

> *Élites do not favour such transfers. They are concerned to improve their capacity through the acquisition of more information and to reinforce their decisive positions through popular support ... Of course, the decision-makers do not eliminate all external views. Rather they operate selectively so that only a limited range of views are heard.*

Reviewing the experiences of the 1980s and early 1990s, Hoggett (1995) confirms this rather pessimistic line of argument:

> *Local political parties of all hues continue to act as if they have a monopoly on democratic power: a basic attitude of distrust prevails towards local citizens' groups who will not or cannot play according to the rules of the local participation game.* (p. 108)

Local authorities only want participation, it is argued, when they can control the process. They do not want to share power.

Many argue, however, that to dismiss officially sponsored public participation is too simplistic. Wilcox (1994), in research for the Joseph Rowntree Foundation, argues that interviews with practitioners involved in promoting participation suggest that a key challenge for government officials is to be clear to the public about what is on offer. Information-giving and formal consultation have a role but they should not be over-sold. Local authorities, however, can and do offer wider and more extensive forms of involvement. Young (1995), in work for the ESRC Local Governance Programme, supports this line of argument on the basis of detailed research into participation in local environmental policy. He notes that many authorities do adopt top-down consultation or limited dialogue strategies. Equally, some local authorities have developed bottom-up strategies which do allow for more extensive public involvement. Viewed from the dizzy heights of the perspective of radical advocates of maximum citizen participation, all officially sponsored schemes will appear inadequate. Those who adopt a less Utopian perspective recognise that although there are limitations, many local officials and councillors are committed to involving the public. Officially sponsored participation is flawed but nevertheless valuable (Gaster, 1995).

Towards a typology of officially sponsored participation
In the following discussion, Young's (1995) three-fold typology of top-down, limited dialogue and bottom-up is developed in order to identify six organisational forms of local officially sponsored participation in the early 1990s. The key criteria is the role of government in the process. As Hogwood (1987) points out, governments can approach the issue of consultation in a variety of ways depending on the firmness of their policy stance.

Top-down strategies start and finish with the initiative with the governmental agencies. The aim is to enhance the position of the authority and gain the confidence and support of the public. There can be an element of negotiation involved. As Hogwood (1987, p. 52) notes, this 'implies that the government does have a view about what it would like to achieve, but is prepared to bargain about the policy to secure the agreement of groups or at least to minimise their opposition'. On the other hand, such top-down strategies can be cosmetic, a matter of going through the motions to be seen to be 'listening'. There would appear to be two broad varieties of such top-down strategies in the local arena. First, there are many examples of formal one-off consultation on policy matters and proposals. Second, in relation to particular services there is a development of consumer-orientated service agreements, with an emphasis on setting performance targets and providing information on service rights to individuals.

Limited dialogue strategies involve a stronger commitment, on the part of the governmental agency, to a two-way process. The initiative for such strategies tends to rest with the governmental agency. The policy framework is set by the governmental agency but the dialogue with the public can lead to substantial change in decisions and thinking. The government is looking not just to legitimate a decision, but for the positive co-operation of outside interests as stakeholders and as potential supporters in the process of implementation. Hogwood (1987, pp. 51–2) notes that in such circumstances governments may be willing to negotiate over the principle or detail of policy. Within the limited dialogue category it is possible to distinguish between two types of approach. First, there are schemes aimed at particular geographical areas, neighbourhood or community forums. Second, there are dialogue approaches which focus on communities of interest. These may involve the users of a particular service or stakeholders interested in a particular policy area or initiative.

Bottom-up strategies are distinguished by their commitment to open discussion and the active encouragement of the involvement of groups which are often excluded or marginalised in decision-making. The policy-making process can be driven by such strategies and the public is provided with an opportunity to take decisions and shape the policy framework. Indeed, Hogwood (1987, p. 50) argues that in such cases 'the government has no clear policy goal, it may act as a referee … Rather than being a direct "combatant", the government is open to competing group bids, though it may prefer the groups themselves to arrive at a consensus and may facilitate the emergence of such a consensus.' Again it is possible to distinguish two organisational varieties under this category. First, there are schemes where the emphasis is on 'visioning', facilitating the identification of priorities and future plans by the public. Second, there are examples of empowerment where disadvantaged groups gain control of a service or policy arena. Community development resources can be vital in ensuring that the unorganised interests can make an impact.

It is not necessary to assume that the strategies identified as 'bottom-up' are better than those described as 'top-down'. As noted earlier in this paper there are a variety of rationale for participation. More pragmatically, Wilcox (1994) argues that it is rather a matter of 'horses for courses'. Different approaches are appropriate at different times and reflect different perceptions of the government's role. To explore the variety of officially sponsored participation, the next sub-sections look at the six-fold categorisation of officially sponsored participation in more detail, especially in the light of recent research material.

Formal consultation

Local authorities have a statutory responsibility to consult the public in relation to some issues, for example land-use planning matters. In addition, they can and do choose to consult about their policy proposals and plans on a discretionary basis. Much of the public participation described by Boaden *et al.* (1982) falls into the category of formal consultation. Young (1995) describes such top-down efforts in the 1990s in the context of preparing Local Agenda 21 in the environmental sphere. Classic activities include such things as writing to local groups, holding public meetings, exhibitions in libraries, touring caravans and newspaper supplements delivered door-to-door. He notes how, compared to earlier initiatives, the local media has been exploited in more sophisticated ways with the use of phone-in programmes. There is much evidence of efforts to ensure that ethnic minorities have access to information through making leaflets available in various languages. In a similar manner, audio cassettes are provided for the blind. The Local Government Commission in England, for example, used all of these techniques, plus opinion polls, in order to gauge public reaction to reorganisation proposals. What it did was regarded as normal practice rather than 'cutting edge' by many local authorities.

Thomas *et al.* (1996) note how Urban Development Corporations (UDCs) along with other agencies of local governance have also engaged in consultation exercises in many cases on an extensive basis. Within the limits of the UDCs' overall mission they note how individual 'community development' officers within UDCs have been given considerable freedom to develop consultation mechanisms. In some instances such officers reported a greater sense of autonomy than they had previously experienced in local authorities. Thomas *et al.* (1996) are careful to point out that the community development units within UDCs have only limited power in their corporate structures. UDC policy may be influenced at the margins but the dominant policy frame remains the achievement of physical renewal in line with central government's objectives and time-scale.

Service agreements

As Boaden *et al.* (1982, p. 170) point out, there are many officials who see participation as a way of improving policies and services by gaining information about what the public wants. Cairncross *et al.* (1994) explore such approaches in relation to housing. They note that compared to the mid-1970s when 42 per cent of local authorities had tenant participation schemes, by the mid-1980s that number had risen to 80 per cent. They identify three types of approach adopted by authorities: traditional, consumerist and citizenship. The first two categories fit into service-focused schemes considered here. Traditional approaches engage in participation in order to gain the confidence and support of their tenants. The underlying aim of the consumerist-approach is the same but it is distinguished by its emphasis on 'market research' and the individual rights of tenants. However, the introduction of competitive tendering into housing management and broader central government policy embodied in the Tenants' Charter has encouraged the incorporation of consumerist thinking into the traditional model.

Estate agreements provide a good example of consumerist service-focused participation. They are based on a negotiated agreement between landlords and tenants of a particular area concerning the standard of service to be provided and forward commitments. Initial research suggests that Estate Agreements do, within the limits of available resources and other constraints, provide a mechanism for tenants to hold their landlord to account in a way that does not demand too much time and effort on their part (Steele *et al.*, 1995).

Cole and Smith (1995) describe an Estate Agreement in York which extended to non-housing matters. They conclude that the Estate Agreement approach is well adapted in principle to the development of local services on a contractual basis. The consumerist revolution that slackened interest in public participation in the early 1980s would appear to provide a platform for some renewed interest in participation by local authorities in the 1990s.

Area-based forums
Area-based forums have a long history in terms of public participation. In urban areas the 1970s saw area management projects; the 1980s was dominated by local authority decentralisation schemes; and the 1990s has seen continued interest in neighbourhood or community-based participation (see Stoker and Young, 1993, Ch. 5 and Lowndes, 1994 for a review). Area forums involve people in a particular community, often alongside councillors and local authority officials, in discussing and responding to policy issues and service needs.

There have been a number of evaluations undertaken by researchers of area-based forums (see in particular Lowndes and Stoker, 1992a and b; Burns *et al.*, 1994). Two themes can be highlighted. First, there is a need for the area scheme to penetrate the wider local authority decision-making structure if it is to maintain the commitment of participants. Second, there is a tendency over time for such organisations to become institutionalised. They become part of the establishment and do not provide a focus for the full range of community interests.

Parish or local councils might also be seen as a focus for area-based participation. Research conducted for the Department of the Environment (Ellwood *et al.*, 1992; Tricker *et al.*, 1993) provides in-depth analysis of their operation. Roughly 30 per cent of the population of England live in areas covered by parish councils. The majority of councils are very small; 49 per cent represent fewer than 500 people. Some councils – particularly those taking the title 'Town Council' – can cover quite large populations. Larger councils tend to provide a more extensive range of services, such as lighting and maintaining footpaths. Many smaller councils also provide some services. However, all sizes of councils are very active in making representations, particularly in relation to planning matters. Only 44 per cent of seats on parish or town councils are contested, although this figure for the late 1980s represents a rise on the position in the mid-1960s. Councils do, however, consult their local community in a variety of ways. Over a quarter in 1989/90, for example, carried out surveys into local needs and concerns.

Interest forums

Another base for two-way dialogue is provided by forums which focus on particular groups of users and those with an interest in a particular topic or issue. Gyford (1996) looks at a range of schemes established up to the mid-1980s. Young (1995) describes the setting up of Environment or Green forums. Many predated the Agenda 21 concern of the early 1990s, but the number has increased since Rio. The central aim of the forums is to bring together a range of stakeholders with an interest in environmental issues. Stewart (1995, pp. 15–19) identifies a range of ways in which local authorities can involve what he calls 'communities of concern'. A range of similar initiatives are described in Gaster and Taylor (1993).

In contrast to the work of decentralisation and area forums, the research on evaluating these schemes is relatively under-developed. Young (1995) notes how the ideas generated by forums can fail to dent the prevailing priorities and perspective of the local authority. Moreover, some representatives are uncomfortable in being seen as representatives for an entire stakeholder category. Forums that are established on a permanent basis run the risk of becoming ossified and institutionalised.

Visioning

Young (1995, p. 4) claims that 'the most important trend in participation in the early 1990s has come in the environmental field where a small number of councils have made a sustained attempt to promote a bottom-up strategy'. He describes the example of Vision 21 in Gloucestershire as typical of the style. Here the County Council contracted Local Agenda 21 participation process to an established local voluntary organisation. A range of sector groups were identified followed by a focus group approach where people 'vision' the future: 'the aim ... is to try and work out the kind of future the participants would like to create, and then to match this as far as possible to the contents of the LA21 document' (pp. 4–5). Further initiatives in Reading, Mendip, Lancashire and Derbyshire are described by Young (1995). The style is similar in many ways to the 'People's Plan' approach pioneered by the Greater London Council in the early 1980s (Brindley *et al.*, 1989, pp. 18–20). Outside the environmental field there are other examples of the visioning strategy. In some circumstances 'village appraisals' in rural areas might be seen as examples of this approach (Hatton, 1995). The 'Planning for Real' techniques pioneered by the Neighbourhood Initiatives Foundation aims to organise local people to produce a consensus about future development proposals. The involvement of users in the preparation of community care plans provides another example (Hoyes *et al.*, 1994). The agenda is relatively open; widespread participation is encouraged and a vision of the future is developed.

The research evaluations of such initiatives suggest that there may be imbalances in those groups that are drawn into the process (Hatton, 1995). The local authority also faces a dilemma about how 'hands-off' is to remain if 'unrealistic' conclusions are drawn (Young, 1995). Hoyes *et al.* (1994) found that in relation to community care, a struggle tends to ensue between the need to deliver a centrally co-ordinated plan and a desire to develop decentralised services and planning systems. Above all for visioning initiatives, the challenge of implementation remains. A 'popular' plan may emerge but it is not easy for the resources for implementation to be found (Brindley *et al.*, 1989).

Empowering the disadvantaged

The final category of 'official' participation is distinguished by its focus on bringing disadvantaged groups into the decision-making process. Geddes (1995, pp. 10–16) describes a range of such initiatives under three headings: urban regeneration, local anti-poverty strategies and quality of public services. Empowering strategies involve a major effort to give socially excluded groups an opportunity to voice their concerns. In particular, projects aim to enhance the capacity of such communities by offering them representation and participation in decision-making forums.

Evaluations of such schemes stress the need for a bottom-up process of community development to accompany empowerment. In a review of the major lessons from the Joseph Rowntree Foundation research programme on 'bringing residents to the centre of regeneration' – which involved 33 studies – Taylor (1995) identifies the following points in relation to participation.

- Solutions and action plans need to start from residents' own priorities; estates are never a blank sheet.

- Innovative techniques and ways of organising discussion can provide a mechanism for traditional non-joiners to participate.

- Residents, as they develop their activity, are likely to need outside support. Training, specialist expertise and dedicated organisational resources may well be necessary.

- Expectations about the capacity of residents to take on the management of service delivery should be kept in check and move at a pace that suits residents.

- Participation requires that other partners respect community views and accept that they may be in conflict with their own.

Substantial levels of community participation and involvement can be achieved though schemes of empowerment (Thomas, 1995; Gibson, 1993). But the difficulties are considerable and it is unwise to expect 'quick-fix' approaches to work – as would appear to have occurred in a number of instances with respect to community involvement in City Challenge schemes (MacFarlane, 1994). As Geddes (1995, p. 11) notes, some examples of sponsorship of community forums can appear to be aimed at undermining critical voices among the disadvantaged by setting up 'tame' community organisations. Empowerment in such circumstances is replaced by a participatory veneer which simply legitimates the decisions of power-holders.

Conclusions

Officially sponsored participation has become a standard element in the process of local decision-making. A range of styles and approaches are discernible. A number of guides to good practice are available which provide an insight into the variety of techniques and methods that are available (see Wilcox, 1994; Stewart, 1995; Young, 1996). Even the standard public meeting can be designed in ways that creates less of an 'us-and-them' divide and provides new opportunities for dialogue (see Stewart, 1995, pp. 23–6 for a description). The key underlying issues for official participation remain: what is the role of government?' Does it have a policy it is seeking endorsement for? Does it want to negotiate? Is it seeking to act as a referee and provide the framework for a participatory 'game' for local interests?

(For recent examples of empowerment strategies see *Local Government Policy Making*, vol. 22, no. 4, March 1996.)

Non-governmental participation

The stimulus to participation does not rest always with government. Citizens in different ways have organised and mobilised in order to demand participation beyond that offered by the ballot box. Community groups and other local interest groups seek to influence the policy process. Studies of such pressure group activity are available, although much of the work is somewhat dated (see Stoker and Wilson, 1991). Some citizen organisations, however, go beyond the immediate defence of their interests to demand changes in the relationship between government and its citizens. In this section of the paper we examine two strands of these non-governmental forces for participation: social movements and Third Force Organisations.

Social movements

Participation is as much a group as an individual activity. One form of citizen involvement that takes a collective form is captured by the term social movement. Examples might include the women's movement, the environmental movement or the peace movement. These movements both express and affect popular consciousness and challenge both the process and outcomes of social and political decision-making. Fainstein and Hirst (1995, pp. 182–3) provide the following definition:

> *Social movements are collective social actors defined by both their (dis)organisation and their aims. Although movements may encompass organisations with dues-payers and membership lists, their overall structure is not fixed and is forever in process of becoming – movements are emergent phenomena. Their aims are always oppositional to established power, but the specific content of their objectives and whether their stance is resistant or transformative, reactionary or progressive, may shift according to their context and internal development.*

Social movements are driven by an 'alternative' world view. They may seek to obtain particular concessions but their objectives transcend such considerations. They challenge the established order in a broad sense by promoting different understandings, values and meanings.

Researchers interested in local politics have focused attention on new social movements, that is movements operating outside the sphere of production and on non-class-based divisions. In particular there is a substantial literature of urban social movements. Such movements are often associated with housing, redevelopment, planning and tax issues. Reviewing the available evidence, Fainstein and Hirst (1995, pp. 197–200) suggest that such organisations have 'expanded the boundaries of local politics ... [and] increased citizen participation in local government and service delivery'. Three factors, however, characterise the development of such movements and indicate limits to their impact (Fainstein and Hirst, 1995, p. 196). First, movements often become absorbed into regular politics and become involved in the administration of government-funded projects. Second, despite their distrust of government such organisations are often reliant on the resources of the public sector to pursue policy objectives. Third, those movements that sustain an intense oppositional stance nevertheless find it hard to establish lasting coalitions with other groups, as would appear to be the case, for example, with respect to the anti-poll tax movement (Burns, 1992).

Research on social movements outside the urban sphere provide empirical support for the general conclusions reached by Fainstein and Hirst. Barnes *et al.* (1995) examine the development of user movements among disabled people and people with mental health problems. Such groups can challenge professional and political judgements and world views at the same time as seeking to influence specific policy objectives and participate in various 'self-help' activities. Legislative changes and the rise of consumerism throughout public services have provided new opportunities and dilemmas for such groups. The development of movements in these areas is a challenge to the previous dominance of charities dominated by the able-bodied and professionals. User movements are a response to exclusion and patronising attitudes. They may also ally themselves to world views that challenge dominant conceptions, advocating instead, for example, a social model of disability. The movement speaks to the shared experiences of exclusion and discrimination and the difficulty in being heard. Its collective organisation is a means to an end but also an end in itself by giving a platform to the previously voiceless.

Abrar (1995) examines the involvement of the women's movement in the development of domestic violence policy in three localities. Only in one case was mobilisation by feminists in the wider community a crucial factor in explaining policy initiatives. In all cases, feminists within governmental institutions played a vital role. As Abrar (1995, p. 27) concludes: 'women's political organising on domestic violence issues is a joint effort and continues to operate across formal and informal boundaries'.

Third Force Organisations

Third Force Organisations (TFOs) is a term that has been used to describe community organisations that are independent of government but which are involved in the implementation of policy. These organisations may attract funds from the public sector as well as other sources. They may engage in protest activity such as social movements but their main focus is on organising provision and projects. Such organisations have existed for over a hundred years – arguably longer – but researchers note that they became increasingly prominent and common from the late 1970s onwards. Resource constraints in the pubic sector have made them attractive to policy-makers. Criticisms of the traditional style of bureaucratic provision have made such organisations attractive to community interests. These push and pull factors have combined to create an environment which has encouraged the development of TFOs.

There are difficulties of definition and terminology with respect to these organisations. Some writers use the general terms voluntary or independent sector, or NGO (non-governmental organisation) but the description Third Force Organisations is preferred because it is more specific (see Young, 1995). These organisations are not part of government or the private sector. They constitute a third force in tackling social and economic challenges. They are community-based organisations that do rather than demand. They are involved in running projects and providing services of their own devising. They run these schemes on a not-for-profit basis and are based in a particular geographical area. Sometimes they are organisations which are run by users for users. On the other hand they can provide services to other groups and interests. They may be relatively informal small organisations or on occasion they may be quite large and more formal (see Taylor *et al.*, 1994). According to Stoker and Young (1993, pp. 121–2), examples of such organisations range from tenants' management co-ops, through organisations running multi-purpose community centres, pre-school playgroups, youth clubs, OAP drop-in centres, to environmental improvement projects.

Young's work on Third Force Organisations constitutes the main attempt to provide an overview of their activities (see Stoker and Young, 1993, Ch. 6; Young, 1995, 1996). It is not possible to do justice to the range of arguments presented by Young. They include the idea of a life cycle for such organisations, an examination of the different types of personnel and leadership involved and an analysis of strategies that are likely to lead to their successful establishment.

Stoker and Young (1993, pp. 129–45) look at the key ingredients of leadership, organisation and access to funds that underlie a successful TFO. Governmental support for such organisations is a delicate and difficult process. A 'key feature of successful TFOs is independence. The essence of this is that the local authority or government agency has to let go' (p. 145).

Clapham and colleagues, in their work for the ESRC Local Governance Programme, provide a rare detailed case study of a small group of successful Third Force Organisations. Their study examines community-based housing organisations (CBHOs) in Glasgow. These organisations were established in the 1980s in several deprived areas to manage and improve small housing estates. The study shows that in contrast to their attitudes to the City Council, the residents receiving a housing service from CBHOs have a very positive attitude to such organisations. They also show a commitment to participation in such organisations which goes beyond the general picture of participation painted in the first section of this paper. Three-quarters of those interviewed had attended a meeting connected to CBHO business in the previous 12 months. There were problems in CBHOs in ensuring the effectiveness of elected representatives both in terms of their contact with other residents and their relationship with full-time salaried staff in the projects. Overall, however, the judgement of the researchers is that the CBHOs in Glasgow have proved to be an extremely successful means of providing services and achieving high levels of satisfaction (see Kintrea, 1995).

Further research is available on the operation of what have been referred to as Third Force Organisations, in work undertaken by the Joseph Rowntree Foundation's Social Care Research Programme (see Taylor *et al.*, 1994; Wilson, 1994) and its work on community regeneration organisations in the housing and urban fields (Thake, 1995; Gibson, 1993; Aldbourne Associates, 1994). Thake and Staubach (1993) indeed, on the basis of their analysis of community-based regeneration initiatives in Germany and the UK, make an argument for a national programme of regeneration resting on the establishment of 200 community enterprise agencies to provide an engine of local capacity building and economic and social renewal. There are, however, as other researchers point out, a number of dilemmas to be faced in trying to create Third Force Organisations on a top-down basis (Stoker and Young, 1993).

Conclusions

Social movements and Third Force Organisations on the surface are very different strands of non-governmental participation. The former express broad, sweeping waves of protest. The latter are concerned with small-scale service provision and projects. However, as Stoker and Young (1993, p. 130) note, the leaders of Third Force Organisations often have had the experience of collective action through social movements. Equally, as Fainstein and Hirst (1995) argue, there is a tendency for social movements to be drawn into service provision by governmental responses to their protests. Moreover, both types of organisation share a scepticism about government and its capacities yet at the same time try to influence its behaviour and draw on its resources. Some advocates of social communitarism may see such organisations as the way forward: the response of civil society to the failings of the state and market. Research suggests the need for some caution. Social movements and TFOs have a complex relationship with government and the latter cannot be stimulated in an easy or simple manner by positive state action.

Research into both aspects of non-governmental participation has produced a number of insights. But compared to other aspects of participation that have been examined thus far, it is in this field that more research is desperately needed, particularly in terms of the role of these organisations and movements in the emerging system of local governance. We know from the available research that an extensive range of activity and projects can be observed, but we do not fully understand the motivation of participants and the dynamics of such organisations. Nor are we in a position to critically assess their impact.

Experimental forms of participation

Stewart (1995, p. 3) argues:

> In recent years local authorities have shown a capacity for innovation in management practice, but little in democratic practice. For the future of local government innovation in democratic practice is at least as important and probably more important than innovation in management practice.

A number of organisations, such as the Commission for Local Democracy (1995), DEMOS (1994) and the Institute of Public Policy Research, have suggested that local authorities should experiment with new forms of participation. This section reviews some of the available research on four major innovative approaches which are not widely practised within British local politics but which have attracted considerable interest. They are:

- the use of referenda and citizens' ballots

- the opportunities provided by information technology

- the development of mechanisms to facilitate deliberative participation.

Referenda and citizens' ballots

Referenda are ballots called on particular issues by government. They are usually advisory but they can be binding. The use of local referenda is common in the United States and Switzerland. Legislation has been introduced recently in a number of European countries to facilitate the holding of local referenda. Cronin (1989) and Caves (1992) provide reviews of the experience in the United States and the Council of Europe has examined experience in Switzerland and elsewhere in Europe. The evidence of these studies suggests that local referenda can stimulate participation and debate. However, there are dangers about some interests gaining undue advantage because of the resources they can bring to public campaigning.

Referenda have a historical role in British local government. Stewart (1995, p. 20) comments that 'once referenda were required before a local authority assumed library powers. Local referenda have been held on licensing issues in Scotland and Wales and used to be held on Sunday opening of cinemas.' Hill (1974) refers to use of polls in relation to a range of matters. More recently referenda have been used only very occasionally and in a highly politicised context. The referendum in Coventry in 1982 about the local rates provides one example. The Strathclyde referendum on water privatisation in 1994 is described in detail in McNulty (1995).

The citizen-initiated ballot has not been practised in Britain at all. This form of direct democratic device is, however, widely employed in other western democracies especially at a local level in the United States (Caves, 1992). Such 'initiatives' as they are called, may be binding or advisory. They require a certain number of signatures of petitioning local citizens for an issue to be placed on a ballot and trigger a vote. At times the local council may respond with a counter-measure of its own on which people can vote. The range of topics covered by such ballots is considerable. Road building, fluoridation, environmental measures and land-use planning matters have all been addressed.

There are a number of issues to be considered in the case of binding citizen ballots: the role of pressure group funding of advertisements, the impact on minority interests, the oversimplification of complex issues. However, it is difficult to deny the freshness that direct democracy approaches could bring to local democracy. Survey evidence indicates a substantial degree of public support and interest in innovations such as referenda and citizens' ballots (Dunleavy and Weir, 1994; Dickson et al., 1995).

The use of information and communication technologies

The opening of the 'information superhighway' provides opportunities for innovation in the practice of local democracy and new possibilities for public participation. The spread of an appropriate infrastructure (cable, fibre optics) and the availability of appropriate hardware (telephone, television, computer and modem) implies that individual householders will have potential access to an array of information from databases and on-line services. In addition, households will be able to communicate with people who have the appropriate information and communication technologies (ITCs). As Percy-Smith (1995, p. 7) notes: 'the new technologies allow the user to move from passive to interactive mode. It is this facility which has given rise to much debate about ICTs and the potential for democracy.'

The new technologies could contribute to an extension of public participation in a variety of ways by:

- facilitating opportunities for direct democracy (televoting)

- providing scope for wide ranging consultation and deliberation on issues

- opening the opportunity for more complex, subtle voting systems to be used in the election of representatives

- making it easier to cast a vote for a representative for those who are housebound

- facilitating the provision of information necessary to accountability

- providing a framework for freedom of speech and association.

Examples of the use of the new technologies in Britain appear to fall into the category of information provision. Western democracies elsewhere do provide some examples of the other uses of the new technologies. Descriptions of the various schemes are provided in Percy-Smith (1995) and DEMOS (1994).

Percy-Smith (1995) provides a useful list of the barriers to be overcome if the democratic aspirations of ICTs are to be met. Two particularly stand out. First, the appropriate ICT infrastructure and hardware is not as yet widespread. It is estimated that by the year 2001 two-thirds of all households will be passed by cable but it is not clear how many will chose to be connected. Currently only about a quarter of households have access to a computer and only a minority of those are connected to the internet. Second, there is an issue about whether people will be overwhelmed by the volume of information that exists and that relatively few will be able to make use of it. She concludes: 'one thing is quite clear – there is no "technological fix" for local democracy and technology should not be allowed to dictate the shape of local politics' (Percy-Smith, 1995, p. 25).

Deliberative forms of participation

Stewart (1995) notes a rise in interest in innovations which are designed to bring into the processes of local government the informed views of citizens. He identifies and describes a range of options: citizens' juries, deliberative opinion polls, consensus conferences, standing citizens' panels and study groups.

The citizens' jury involves an adoption of the jury system used in trials for the consideration of policy issues. A representative sample of residents are drawn together and asked to provide recommendations about a policy issue. Their deliberation takes place over a reasonable period of time and is informed by expert advice, data and administrative support.

Stewart et al. (1994) provide a detailed review of the experience of such juries in the United States and elsewhere in Europe. They describe some successful schemes but note that to run juries effectively can involve substantial public spending to underwrite the jurors' loss of earnings, and other costs. Moreover, the process of deliberation within the jury is not without problems and difficulties in terms of the capacity of the jurors to use the information provided and not be subject to manipulation. Further, when the jury's findings are reported they may be distorted by the media or by other interests in the policy process. Stewart et al. (1994, p. vi) nevertheless conclude: 'citizens' juries can be seen as enriching rather than supplanting representative democracy'. They call for a range of experiments with juries. This call has been taken up by the Local Government Management Board and a range of local initiatives have been developed (reported in *Municipal Journal*, 5 July 1996, pp. 21–2).

Deliberative opinion polls have in particular been advocated by Fishkin (1991). In effect these are opinion polls undertaken after a public airing of the issues so that voters are more likely to make an informed choice. Multi-choice referenda provide another option. Elkin (1987, p. 173) argues for such polls to be introduced into decision-making in American cities.

Referenda items can be written so that citizens must pick from among several responses, each of which both lays out a reason for picking that response and denotes intensity of feeling. The important point about the referenda is that citizens are induced to think about the reasons for their votes.

The different initiatives described by Stewart (1995) all rest on developing deliberation as a crucial element in decision-making. Citizens' juries and deliberative opinion polls provide rather high profile mechanisms for developing deliberation. Some of the other measures such as study circles and citizens' panels are more low key; nevertheless, they can provide scope for informed citizen input into the decision-making process. There are a number of studies of such panels in operation providing opportunities for service users to find a voice for their concerns (Barnes *et al.*, 1994).

Conclusions

The research work on experimental forms of participation is relatively undeveloped for obvious reasons. Yet there is a strong argument for it to move from descriptive to a more analytic and evaluative form. If such a move was made there is scope for a worthwhile partnership between initiatives on the ground and research. The potential for such forms of participation to provide new strands to a pluralist vision of democracy is difficult to deny. They are not necessarily a replacement for traditional forms of representative and participatory democracy but direct and deliberative schemes, combined with the potential offered by new technologies, offer new challenges for local politics.

Concluding comments

The research work on local political participation has many strengths. The ESRC and the Department of the Environment have funded a number of studies that provide insights into the background or infrastructure of participation. The Local Government Management Board and the Joseph Rowntree Foundation have stimulated a range of studies into the practice of participation and have sought to draw lessons out as to how that practice might be improved. The interest of the Commission for Local Democracy in public participation has provided further stimulus to work in the field.

There, as ever, remains scope for further work in this area. The research on non-governmental forms of participation is less well-developed than that on official schemes. Further research work on social movements and Third Force Organisations would be highly desirable. We need to know more about how such institutions work. As for officially sponsored schemes there is an argument for more in-depth and long-term evaluation studies. Of course many officially sponsored participation initiatives have only a limited life-span. What would be worthwhile is an analysis aimed at examining the cumulative impact of such schemes within a locality. Has two decades of officially sponsored projects created a sustainable participation infrastructure? If not, why not ?

At several stages in this review paper the potential for locality effects has been identified in, for example, both the rates of participatory activity and the practice of local voting. What is it beyond social and economic characteristics that appears to make some local political systems more supportive of participation than others? Is it possible to discover a local form of organising politics that encourages greater participation?

Finally, the developing work on what has been designated as experimental forms of participation needs to be continued, preferably in tandem with initiatives on the ground. The interest in more direct and deliberative forms of democracy demands a research response that does not take a rose-tinted view of such developments but seeks instead to provide a critical assessment of their scope and limitations.

References

Abrar, S. (1995) 'Feminist intervention and the adoption of domestic violence policy at the local level', paper to the ESRC Local Governance Programme Conference, Exeter, 19–20 September

Aldbourne Associates (1994) *The Feasibility of 'Residents' Democracy*, Housing Research Findings 133. York: JRF

Barber, B. (1984) *Strong Democracy.* Berkeley: University of California Press

Barnes, M., Cormie, J. and Crichton, M. (1994*) Seeking Representative Views from Frail Older People.* Kirkcaldy: Age Concern Scotland

Barnes, M., Harrison, S., Mort, M., Shardlow, P. and Wistow, G. (1995) 'Consumers, citizens and officials: new relationships in health and social care?', paper to ESRC Local Governance Conference, Exeter

Beetham, D. (1996) 'Local government and democracy', in D. King and G. Stoker (eds) *Rethinking Local Democracy.* London: Macmillan

Boaden, N., Goldsmith, M., Hampton, W. and Stringer, P. (1982) *Public Participation in Local Services.* Harlow: Longman

Brindley, T., Rydin, Y. and Stoker, G. (1989) *Remaking Planning*. London: Unwin Hyman

Burns, D. (1992) *Poll Tax Rebellion*. London: AK Press and Attack International

Burns, D., Hambleton, R. and Hoggett, P. (1994) *The Politics of Decentralisation*. London: Macmillan

Cairncross, L., Clapham, D. and Goodlad, R. (1994) 'Tenant participation and tenant power in British council housing', *Public Administration*, vol. 72, no. 2, pp. 177–200

Caves, R. (1992) *Land Use Planning. The Ballot Box Revolution*. Newbury Park, California: Sage

Cohen, J. (1989) 'Deliberation and democratic legitimacy', in A. Hamlin and P. Pettit (eds) *The Good Polity*. Oxford: Basil Blackwell

Cole, I. and Smith, Y. (1995) *From Estate Action to Estate Agreement*, Housing Research Findings 159. York: JRF

Commission for Local Democracy (1995) *Taking Charge: The Rebirth of Local Democracy*. London: Municipal Journal Books

Cronin, T. (1989) *Direct Democracy*. Harvard: Harvard University Press

Curtice, J. and Jowell, R. (1995) 'The sceptical electorate', in R. Jowell *et al.* (ed.) *British Social Attitudes – the 12th Report*. London: SCPR Dartmouth

DEMOS (1994) 'Lean democracy', *Demos Quarterly*, 3

Dickson, M. (1995) 'Seeing Us How Others See Us: Comparative Public and Elite Attitudes to Local Governance', ESRC Local Governance Conference, Exeter

Dunleavy, P. and Weir, S. (1994) 'Citizens and town halls', *Local Government Chronicle*, 29 April, p. 12

Elkin, S. (1987) *City and Regime in the American Republic*. Chicago: University of Chicago Press

Ellwood, S., Nutley, S., Tricker, M. and Waterston, P. (1992) *Parish and Town Councils in England: A Survey*. London: HMSO

Fainstein, S. and Hirst, C. 'Urban social movements', in D. Judge, G. Stoker and H. Wolman (1995) (eds) *Theories of Urban Politics*. London: Sage

Fishkin, J. (1991) *Democracy and Deliberation*. Newhaven: Yale University Press

Gaster, L. (1995) 'Managing a localised democratic process: an optimist's view', ESRC Local Governance Programme Workshop, October

Gaster, L. and Taylor, M. (1993) *Learning from Consumers and Citizens*. Luton: LGMB

Geddes, M. (1995) *Poverty, Excluded Communities and Local Democracy*. London: Commission for Local Democracy

Gibson, T. (1993) *Estates Regeneration an Meadowell*, Housing Research Findings 97. York: JRF

Gyford, J. (1996) Committee of Inquiry into the Conduct of Local Authority Business *Research Volume IV: Aspects of Local Democracy*, Cmnd 9801. London: HMSO

Hague, R., Harrop, M. and Breslin, S. (1992) *Comparative Government and Politics* Third Edition. London: Macmillan

Hain, P. (1980) *Neighbourhood Participation*. London: Temple Smith

Hatton, V. (1995) 'Public participation in village appraisals', paper presented to the Planning and Housing Conference, Herriot Watt University, 27–29 June

Hill, D. (1970) *Participating in Local Affairs*. Harmondsworth: Penguin

Hill, D. (1974) *Democratic Theory and Local Government*. London: Allen and Unwin

Hoggett, P. (1995) 'Does local government want local democracy?', *Town and Country Planning*, vol. 64, no. 4 , April, pp. 107–9

Hogwood, B. (1987) *From Crisis to Complacency? Shaping Public Policy in Britain.* Oxford: University Press

Horton, M. (1967) *Committee in the Management of Local Government: Volume 3: The Local Government Elector.* London: HMSO

Hoyes, L., Lart, R., Means, R. and Taylor, M. (1994) *User Empowerment and the Reform of Community Care,* Social Care Research Findings 50. York: JRF

Jones, G. and Stewart, J. (1985) *The Case for Local Government* (second edition). London: Allen and Unwin

Kintrea, K. (1995) 'Sustainability and maturity of community-based housing organisations', paper presented to Housing Studies Association Conference, Edinburgh, September

Lowndes, V. (1994) Special issue of *Local Government Policy Making*

Lowndes, V. and Stoker, G. (1992a) 'An evaluation of neighbourhood decentralisation: customer and citizen perspectives', *Policy and Politics,* vol. 20, no. 1, pp. 47–61

Lowndes, V. and Stoker, G. (1992b) 'An evaluation of neighbourhood decentralisation: staff and councillor perspectives', *Policy and Politics,* vol. 20, no. 2, pp. 143–152

Lynn, P. (1992) *Public Perceptions of Local Government: Its Finance and Services.* London: HMSO

MacFarlane, R. (1994) *Community Involvement in City Challenge,* Housing Research Findings 105. York: JRF

Macnaughton, P. (1995) *Public Perceptions and Sustainability in Lancashire: Indicators, Institutions, Participation.* Preston: Lancashire County Council

McNulty, D. (1995) *Referenda and Citizens' Ballots.* London: Commission for Local Democracy

Miller, W. (1986) 'Local electoral behaviour', in Committee of Inquiry into the Conduct of Local Authority Business *Research Volume III: The Local Government Elector.* London: HMSO

Miller, W. (1988) *Irrelevant Elections? The Quality of Local Democracy in Britain*. Oxford: Clarendon Press

Moyser, G., Parry, G. and Day, N. (1992) *Political Participation and Democracy in Britain*. Cambridge: Cambridge University Press

Mulgan, G. (1994) *Politics in an Antipolitical Age*. Cambridge: Polity Press

Newton, K. (1976) *Second City Politics*. Oxford: Clarendon Press

Parry, G., Moyser, G. and Day, N. (1992) *Political Participation and Democracy in Britain*. Cambridge: Cambridge University Press

Percy-Smith, J. (1995) *Digital Democracy: Information and Communication Technologies in Local Politics*. London: Commission for Local Democracy

Phillips, A. (1994) *Local Democracy: the Terms of the Debate*. London: Commission for Local Democracy

Phillips, A. (1995) *The Politics of Presence*. Oxford: Clarendon Press

Rallings, C. and Thrasher, M. (1994) *Explaining Election Turnout*. London: HMSO

Rallings, C., Temple, M. and Thrasher, M. (1994*) Community and Participation in Local Democracy*. London: Commission for Local Democracy

Royal Commission on Local Government in England (1969) *Community Attitudes Survey*: England Research Studies 9. London: HMSO

Steele, A., Sommerville, P. and Galvin, G. (1995) *The Effectiveness of Estate Agreements* Housing Research Findings 160. York: JRF

Stewart, J. (1995) *Innovation in Democratic Practice*. Birmingham: INLOGOV

Stewart, J., Kendal, E. and Coote, A. (1994) *Citizens' Juries*. London: Institute of Public Policy Research

Stoker, G. and Wilson, D. (1991) 'The lost world of British local pressure groups', *Public Policy and Administration,* vol. 16, no. 2, pp. 285–302

Stoker, G. and Young, S. (1993) *Cities in the 1990s*. Harlow: Longman

Taylor, M. (1995) *Unleashing the Potential: Bringing Residents to the Centre of Regeneration*, Housing Summary 12. York: JRF

Thake, S. (1995*) The Effect of Community Regeneration Organisations on Neighbourhood Regeneration*, Housing Summary 10 (with supplement). York: JRF

Thake, S. and Staubach, R. (1993) *Investing in People*. York: JRF

Thomas, D. (1995) *A Review of Community Development*, Social Policy Summary 5. York: JRF

Thomas, H., Brownhill, S., Razzaque, K. and Stirling, T. (1996) *Local Governance and Race Equality*, Final Report to ESRC Local Governance Programme

Tricker, M., Collingridge, J., Gosling, P., Green, J., Hems, L., Mills, L., Soni, S. and Waterston, P. (1993) *Roles and Activities of Parish and Town Councils in England: Case Studies*. London: HMSO

Wilcox, D. (1994*) Community Participation and Empowerment: Putting Theory Into Practice*, Housing Summary 4. York: JRF

Wilson, D. and Game, C. (1994) *Local Government in the United Kingdom*. London: Macmillan

Wilson, J. (1994) *Self Help Groups and Professionals*, Social Care Research Findings 60. York: JRF

Young, K. (1986) 'Attitudes to local government', in Committee of Inquiry into the Conduct of Local Authority Business *Research Volume III: The Local Government Elector*. London: HMSO

Young, K. and Rao, N. (1995) 'Faith in local democracy', in R. Jowell and J. Curtice (eds) *British Social Attitudes: The Twelfth Report*. Aldershot: Gower

Young, S. (1995) 'Participation: trends and prospects in the environmental sphere', paper to the ESRC Local Governance Programme Conference, Exeter

Young, S. (1996) 'Promoting participation and community-based partnerships in the context of Local Agenda 21', unpublished paper